A SCIENTIST

JOURNEY OF A VILLAGE BOY OF BIHAR, BHARAT (INDIA)

Sushant Singh

Clever Fox
PUBLISHING

Chennai • Bangalore

CLEVER FOX PUBLISHING
Chennai, India

Published by CLEVER FOX PUBLISHING 2023
Copyright © Sushant Singh 2023

All Rights Reserved.
ISBN: 978-93-56483-41-5

HOW TO GET THE BEST OUT OF THIS BOOK

Scientists are not dropped from space; they are like other normal humans, meaning that an individual's upbringing, inherited characteristics, and sincere efforts to evolve as a better human being will help shape the kind of human they become. Consequently, that will determine what kind of scientists they become. Also, the country's history, culture, socioeconomic and political progression significantly impact them. Therefore, readers should not assume that becoming a scientist is a journey completed in a few years of academic and research experiences. Instead, the texts in this book should be considered merely as an abstract of a more extensive experience that has spanned over as little as three decades. Therefore, it is advised to research further to fill all the gaps readers may discover while reading this book. The challenges discussed in this book are grave but presented in diluted forms; therefore, do not underestimate them. However, this should not be taken as demotivation. Ultimately, the book provides various dimensions of the society a scientist lives in for informed decision-making by readers.

MOTIVATION

I grew up in a humble family in a village in the Begusarai district of Bihar in India. My grandparents had no formal education and lived in a mud-made house in the early stages of their life. My journey started from that village and took me to the United States of America (USA) for higher studies, i.e., to earn a Ph.D. degree. In this long journey, several Sushants crossed my way, or maybe a better version of Sushant that I felt lacked motivation, commitment, guidance, and resources. I also learned about many potential scientists who could not complete their Ph.D. studies and dropped 4-5 years of hard work without completing their Ph.D. degrees for various reasons, primarily because they lacked support from their advisors.

I believe that my Guru, Lord Shiva, and Goddess Saraswati have been very kind to me, and that is why despite several challenges, I earned two Ph.D. degrees, one in India and another in the USA.

With this book, I hope to reach out to at least one other Sushant and inspire him/her to never give up on their dream to be a scientist or pursue science for any reason and to never let the "Scientist" in them die. Furthermore, I want to convey that you should never abandon your hard work and passion for pursuing science, regardless of whatever challenges you may encounter. The success of this book depends on how many such Sushants get motivated to do and live science despite several challenges they may encounter.

"We may not receive what we aspire for, so we better start loving what we are provided with. Science is not done in laboratories only; it is everywhere, depending on whether we have learned and understood science well and how, where, and when to apply it."

DISCLAIMER

Writing a book on our own life is not easy. So, I want to be very clear that the sole purpose of this book is only to motivate deserving students who aspire to be a scientist. There were several challenges I may have encountered during this journey, but my intent here is not to share those stories or incidences that may knowingly or unknowingly create any controversy or discomfort in anyone's life.

I did have several challenges in this journey. However, my philosophy has been straightforward: whenever we are dragged into a battle, we decide whether to surrender to the challenges or to stand, fight, and win. Unfortunately, I decided to walk on the latter path; consequently, I was mentally prepared to get wounded. So, my humble request to readers is that they see if they find something positive about my journey that may inspire them to have firm determination to achieve the goals they have aspired for.

"There is no shortcut to becoming a scientist. To be a good scientist, one needs to understand, assimilate, and live science in every bit of life; then, only one can become a good scientist; otherwise, only earning a Ph.D. degree will not help them, science, or society."

ACKNOWLEDGEMENTS

I want to respect the identity and privacy of those who supported me in my journey to becoming a scientist. I would not use anybody's name without their consent, so I may only indicate them as a third person. I want to extend my heartiest thanks to my family, friends, and mentors in India and the USA who trusted me and supported me unconditionally throughout my journey to becoming a scientist. I am also thankful to all my collaborators; without their support, I would not have been able to expand my research works.

"There is an imbalanced population of good and evil souls on this earth, the latter dominates, but the former always wins; never get disheartened if evil souls surround you; good spirits are out there to support you."

LIST OF PHOTOGRAPHS

CONTENTS

Contents

FAMILY
BACKGROUND

There are some things in life that none of us will ever get, yet there is always a purpose behind everything that comes our way. I have also realized that no one will always be lucky or pampered, nor will they constantly be on the receiving end of misfortune. Nevertheless, we can use the rocks that life throws at us to construct a brick wall that will be impregnable and eventually become a strong fortress. I had no choice but to live my life this way as it was the only survival skill I could afford to acquire.

My family was middle class, and we lived in a village in India called Hajipur Pipra Dewas, of Barauni Block of the Begusarai District in Bihar. My family was of the ordinary, average kind that one might come across in any given village. However, my mother and father are both well-educated, with my father holding a degree in agriculture. He started working for the state government as an employee after completing his studies and since then he has maintained an impeccable track record.

My family line was built on a set of firm core beliefs and principles that stayed with us all for years and that we were positive would be passed on to our upcoming children. These values and principles include: my parents followed in their parent's footsteps by making many concessions to ensure that their children, including my father, would have a good education and a secure financial future. They, in turn, made sure that they did not leave any stone unturned to ensure that all their hopes and dreams for a better life for us were realized. They sacrificed their conveniences to improve our standard of living and educational opportunities.

My other two family members are my older brother and my younger sister; I am the middle child. My older brother, younger sister, and I started our childhoods during times when our parents were going through incredibly humbling moments. However, none of us were prevented from obtaining the necessities of life. My parents put every bit of the money they worked so hard to earn into our health and education. They might not have had the whole world at their fingers, but even with what they did have, they made the most of it. They ensured that we placed high importance on contentment early in our lives. Even though they tried very hard to make our childhood as pleasant as possible, I have no hesitation in asserting that they placed just as much emphasis on our moral education as they did on our academic and intellectual development.

While my grandfather learned his signature, my paternal grandparents were illiterate. However, they made it a point to encourage all their grandchildren and great-grandchildren to get educated. Even though my maternal grandparents could read and write, there were never any bumps in the road in the relationship that both families shared.

In Indian culture and tradition, Goddess Saraswati is known for knowledge, learning, and wisdom. Our grandmother always taught us to respect knowledge and seek blessings from Goddess Saraswati so that we could succeed and become intellectual souls. Our first teacher, our mother, complimented that motivation by instilling a good routine, spending enough time on education, and respecting knowledge and wisdom. It was only because of our mother's teachings did we started our primary education in one of the best schools in the town at that time.

My experience has taught me that there is much more to a child's upbringing than what they wear, eat, and the words they hear. The kinds of societies that are conducive to the development of healthy children and the degree to which the environment in which children are raised is safe are significant factors. Our mother ensured we became good humans, earned good education, avoided bad habits, and succeeded. She also made sure that we inherited humans' core elements, including humility, honesty, hard work, dedication, and empathy for people in need.

It was pretty evident to us–my siblings and me–early enough that it was up to us to create a life and future for ourselves better than our parents could afford. We were content but also determined. Amongst the challenges that rocked my childhood, a few handfuls entirely shaped me and contributed to the force that motivated me to become a scientist. Before rounding up this chapter, let me share a few of the core values and principles that I learned thanks to the upbringing I had.

1.1. Determination

As much as we were not entirely well-to-do family, my parents ensured that we never saw ourselves as lesser than our wealthier friends, colleagues, and neighbors. They also ensured that we built a sense of self-consciousness and a strong will to create a beautiful future for ourselves. Determination is not a mere wish to do or achieve something. It is a quality that separates those who achieve their goals from those who quit and keep making many excuses as to why things are impossible.

Even when we are disadvantaged—such as how I was born into a family of little or no societal privileges—it is very typical to have a strong urge to quit, but a determined soul would remain focused on the goal and pay no heed to the surrounding circumstances. Being determined would also help one overcome the unexpected, develop self-respect, and grow stronger.

"My parents made my siblings and me little warriors by making us realize these determination facts early in life: it helped us; it helped me, and it can help others too."

1.2. Hard work and Honesty

It is most likely untrue when anything is too good to be true: this kept ringing in my mind whenever I saw people take shortcuts and found them almost tempted to relinquish their integrity. The truth is that when we get hungry for anything, we tend to seek any means possible to get it done, whether it is immoral or legal. To protect our emotions and guard ourselves against temptations, our parents deemed it fit to engrave the beauty of discipline and hard work into our hearts at a very young age.

"As opposed to the social realities we are constantly exposed to, we need to remember that we need to work hard and there is no shortcut. If we do, we do not need to worry about the results. If our efforts are sincere and honest, they will bring good outcomes; if not, continue the hard work and learn from previous mistakes."

Our parents also looked at our sincere efforts and not our grades in our exams. These were not mere words; we saw them demonstrated every day.

1.3. Financial Saving

Money is never enough for us; by nature, it is volatile. It keeps flowing from one person to another and from one place to another. Therefore, people should learn how to save money when it is with us. Saving is a habit, but not due to having enough money to save. Our mother consistently demonstrated this habit of saving. We never knew how much our father earned or how we got everything we needed daily.

As mentioned in the previous section, my father did not have a high-paying job, but my mother has been an outstanding financial manager. I have been very close to my mother and learned several things from her. I still remember there was a time when our father did not receive his salary for 18 months. There was no support from anyone. Our mother never let us feel that we were in crisis. She managed very well, and I believe she was blessed because even today, it gives us goosebumps thinking how a family of five people survived when their regular income was halted for 18 months. Our mother also taught us never to take a loan because it becomes a habit, and we get trapped. She still gives us money whenever we travel outside. We never understood how she managed to save money without compromising all our needs. Over time, although the family size has increased with the addition of the next generation of kids, our mother continued to make sure everybody's needs are fulfilled.

We also remember she never hesitated to attend social events and offer good gifts. So, the expenses were not only in the family, but a significant amount of funds flowed into society. She may not have received good gifts, but she made sure the gifts she offered were of good quality, and the recipients could use them. She kept saying that we should not change our character according to people; if you give something to someone, it should be helpful to the recipient, and you should give it with respect. All these incidents and conversations had a significant impact on us.

One way, saving money is a habit. Some other habits may cost us money and health. I had no bad habits, so I had no extra expenses. I never got influenced by money, glamour, or anything with any physical or monetary value. Therefore, I never spent much money on anything other than my basic needs. This helped me save money to help myself and others when needed.

"If God made you capable of helping someone, you should help people in need wherever possible, with no expectation of getting the money or any favor back."

If my support to others were fruitful, I felt good, and if not, then I tried to take it as if I owed someone in my past life, so I had to repay them in this life. Therefore, even if we do not think of others to lead a good peaceful life, we should have this habit of saving money and resources and instill the same in the following generations.

1.4. Empathy

Empathy is the ability to emotionally understand other people's feelings, see things from their point of view, and imagine yourself in their place. Essentially, it is putting yourself in someone else's position and feeling what they must be feeling. For example, when you see another person suffering, you might be able to instantly envision yourself in their place and feel sympathy for what they are going through. Sympathy and empathy are not skills that can be learned; they are natural traits. It is also an integral part of our culture, practices, and surroundings. I would say that this human characteristic came naturally to me due to my parents' influence. While people are generally well-attuned to their feelings and emotions, getting into someone else's head can be more complicated. The ability to feel empathy allows people to "walk a mile in another's shoes," so to speak. It permits people to understand the emotions that others are feeling. Seeing another person in pain and responding with indifference or outright hostility seems utterly incomprehensible to many. Nevertheless, the fact that some people respond in such a way demonstrates that empathy is not necessarily a universal response to the suffering of others.

"The core thought is that to be empathetic, you should not be rich or powerful; you must be sensitive and sensible to others."

Time changes, as do the situations; therefore, being sympathetic to others makes us truly human. I am not sure how the readers will find the following: I supported many people whom I knew came to me with an agenda of getting benefits and going away, but my thoughts were that they came to me when they were in need, even if their intentions were not positive, I must help them. What they took away from me were money, time, and emotions. However, nothing made me become a person with a stone heart.

"Your parents are the best; they do everything to nurture you well. So, never compare yourself or your parents to others. Instead, get the best out of whatever resources you have."

EDUCATION

2.1. The Foundation

My academic journey was anything but a breeze at any point in time. Because my father's employment location was transferrable and the state's regulation mandated that he move to a new city every three years, I had no choice but to attend a new school every three years, just like a true gypsy. My educational journey started at the Prabhat Tara School, a Christian missionary school in the Muzaffarpur district of Bihar in India. At that time, it was widely regarded as one of the most reputable educational institutions in the city. Because of the school's long history of academic success, many parents considered it their top option when selecting a learning institution for their children. However, I still remember that school has a significant population of kids, mainly from affluent families and people in high-ranked positions. Therefore, getting accepted into the school was difficult because there were so many applicants each year, and the school only had a limited number of application slots.

Consequently, the school was quite competitive. I remember how my mother had to personally prepare my elder brother and me for the entrance papers for us to do well enough on the tests we were given to be accepted into the kindergarten program at that school. Both my brother and I secured admission to that school. The school had good teachers, discipline, and extra-curricular activities. The school also had a zoo inside the campus. Even today, it is hard to imagine that I studied in such a school. Unfortunately, after those first three years, my father received a transfer to another city, and we had to switch schools.

The next city my father got relocated to was a century behind the rest of the globe. Hence, he believed it would be in the family's best interest to have us stay in our paternal village until he transferred to a better workplace. So, my brother and I quickly bagged admission into the village's government primary school, where we completed our primary education.

It took us a very long time, but we ultimately obtained our certificate of primary education. Unfortunately, the setting for learning was not favorable to success. The situation was so awful that we did not have a table or a bench to sit and study. As a result, we had to bring a jute mat to school to fulfill this purpose. Aside from these considerations, the instructors gave their all to instill information in us. A few months after we completed our elementary education in the countryside, my father was transferred again, this time to the Katihar region, a much better city than the previous location.

My parents ensured that our schoolwork proceeded smoothly the entire time we traveled. After settling down, we went to the appropriate authorities to register and then started attending Hari

Shankar Nayak High School, a government school for class sixth to tenth education located in the Katihar district of Bihar. One more time, I want to pay tribute to my parents for their conscious efforts to provide us with a high-quality education to the best of their abilities. At Hari Shankar Nayak High School, the teachers were fantastic, and we were given various opportunities to compete in various sports and sporting activities.

When I was in ninth grade, we were forced to relocate to Madhepura, another city in Bihar. Because of this process, I had to throw about half of my studies out the window. My preparations for the tenth board exam, which was waiting for me, needed to begin immediately.

In Madhepura, there was a school in the neighborhood where our home was located. I witnessed pupils engaging in dishonest behavior via cheating during school tests. They used to have assistance from members of their family who lived elsewhere. My encounter with it was novel and unexpected. My father enquired which school I would choose to go to take the tenth-grade board exam. I could have gone to Madhepura or stayed in my hometown and studied there. However, I did not feel at ease with the approach that Madhepura took to conduct exams. Furthermore, my home community had an utterly foreign school, a different school located a couple of kilometers away from where I lived. Despite this, I decided to take my tenth board exam from that government school.

Life is dynamic and multiple things continue happening at the same time. I realized this when we went through one of the worst phases of our life when we lost our grandfather. He did not survive long after his retirement and died because of health issues. However, he has been our inspiration and an ideal man. He had a lovely and strong personality but was also kind-hearted. I experienced his courage in both official and social settings. He was and still is our idol. Losing him was like losing the whole world. We remember him every day in our life. We believe that whatever we achieve is because of his blessings and the excellent Sanskar he and our grandmother were able to transfer to us.

I do not know how, but I finished ninth grade at that school and kept studying for the standardized test in tenth grade. I was only able to study for the entirety of my tenth-grade year. The instructors at this government school were outstanding, particularly the ones who taught biology and economics. I suppose this was probably when I became so interested in Biology. When I was in school, the biology teacher drew many illustrations on the blackboard to exemplify different concepts and theories related to biology. My economics instructor was also of the highest caliber. Both topics were interesting, but I became more interested in biology.

I worked hard to get through two years' worth of material in only one year. My grandmother was integral to this process and played an important role. It was usually around four in the morning when she woke me up so that I could study and review the material again. Finally, the exam day arrived, and I took the board exam for tenth grade. During the test, I noticed several kids cheating, but not as flagrantly as I had seen at Madhepura. As a student, I had the habit of writing down what I learned for exams, and even if I did not obtain outstanding scores, I was confident that I would at least place in the top division. However, most of us were in for a surprise when we least expected it. The examination authorities gave all the examinees average or very conservative results because there were multiple reports of students cheating on the examinations. After a few months, the exam results were presented in a published form. I needed to check my grades, so I went to school. Unfortunately, despite having the second-highest score in the class, I could not advance to the first level. Since I began my studies, this was the first time I received a score in the second division. Undoubtedly, it was a big disappointment for me, but I cannot only blame the authorities; I was probably not 100% prepared for this exam.

On that day, my father was at the village home; I was not only depressed but also anxious. I smiled bitterly as I reached home. Outside the home, my father and a few other people could be seen sitting. My father inquired about my result. I responded by saying that I could only get the second division.

"It's okay," he assured me, "there is no need to be concerned about that. Have you accomplished what you set out to do?"

I responded, "Not really, but not too far," because I was only a few points away from making it to the first level.

"That's fine," he told me, "Take it easy." That was a moment of realization for me. My parents never once pressured us to achieve good scores. They did not require anything more of us other than honest labor and effort.

We were still living in Madhepura when I passed the tenth grade, meaning we had not moved. My father's job allowed him to continue working from Madhepura, so our family was spared from the inconvenience of relocating to a new city this time. I decided to continue my education beyond the 10th grade by enrolling at the Thakur Prasad (T.P.) College in Madhepura, a public college, which at one time was one of the most prestigious educational institutions in the region. I found out during the first session of college that I was the only one in the classroom to have received a second division in 10th grade. The rest of the students in the room were far ahead of me regarding the grades they received in 10th grade. The fact that a particular introductory course did not have much of an effect on me is something for which I am grateful to my teachers. They did not emphasize academic performance in the 10th board exam. When I think back to those teachers, I can confidently claim that many of them were on the same level as the best teachers in the world. Their knowledge, manner of instruction, personality, and willingness to assist students are all unrivaled up until this point. I finished 12th grade, also known as an intermediate school, with a focus on biology and mathematics. I was able to place in the first division.

2.2. Moment of the Decision

In our society in India, once we complete 12th grade, that is the time to decide the choices of occupation, so the next obstacle to overcome is selecting a career path.

If we want to go forward in life after graduating from college, we must think carefully about the professional path we want to take. This is a critical choice to make, and it may be challenging to choose which is more suitable based on your requirements. While the degree program we pick is essential, completing it is just the beginning of the process. When it comes to choosing the best job path that will be helpful in the future, college students may face a few crucial challenges. One of these issues is choosing the right career. When choosing a future occupation, two of the most common errors that young people make are imitating the actions of others and failing to obtain sufficient guidance.

College is supposed to be a time when students get the support and guidance they need to make meaningful life choices. Unfortunately, the necessary counseling and career coaching will not be accessible to all students to the same extent. Because of this, it may be challenging for them to find a line of work that will allow them to progress in life. A student would be missing a critical opportunity to learn about the numerous alternatives available to them depending on their preferences if they did not receive enough career counseling while they were still in school. They could be under the impression that they only have one or two options and feel disheartened if none appeal to them. As a result of the fact that a significant number of students do not receive the necessary assistance with their careers, it is common for these students to act hastily when faced with a decision because they are on their own.

Consequently, college students frequently choose a subject for their major based solely on the fact that they have a personal connection to someone else in the field. Many students are under the impression that the degree they are pursuing is not nearly as significant as it is, even though it is intended to correspond to the kind of work they would like to do in the future. They find themselves completely engulfed in the crowd and choose to do what everyone else is doing without considering how it will impact them before it is too late. In this regard, my story was not too different from other students.

After completing 12th grade, several of my friends settled on pursuing engineering careers, but I wanted to be a medical doctor. My decision to become a medical doctor was inspired by several factors, including my fascination with biology, my father's ambition to work in medicine, and my grandfather's passing due to a slight paralytic attack.

Even though I wanted to pursue a medical career, I always had a backup plan in mind. Consequently, my alternative strategy was to earn at least a bachelor's degree. I enrolled in an undergraduate program at the T. P. College in Madhepura. I was also preparing for the medical admission exam parallelly. When choosing the principal (honors) subject for my undergraduate class, I was in a tough predicament regarding which subject to select. My zoology instructor was excellent, and I learned a lot from him. I excelled in the practical aspects of the subject, such as laboratory experiments and dissections. I was also interested in Zoology. However, because most of my close friends chose Botany as their primary study area, I did the same thing so that I would not be left out. My Zoology professor was distressed when I told him about my decision. I, too, was unhappy with the situation, but had no other option. I do not know whether it was a right or wrong decision, but Zoology was my first choice as the Professor trained me well, and I was very good at zoology laboratory work. Regardless, I did my best in Botany.

Parallelly, I gave the test for admission to medical school twice but could not achieve a score that met the requirements. Both exams were missed by a total of 3 and 2 numbers, respectively. I did get accepted into a physiotherapy program, but I ultimately chose not to pursue that line of work because, at that time, it was not a particularly well-liked profession. Due to all these factors, I stopped studying for the medical admission exams and instead started concentrating on my undergraduate studies. I could have tried a couple more times for medical exams, but I did not have the privilege to afford another year. Therefore, I started focusing on my undergraduate degree and getting private botany lessons from one of our college's best teachers. I believe that it was around this stage that I concluded that since I would not be able to become a medical doctor, I would instead pursue a Ph.D. degree which would allow me to satisfy that motivation while still serving society through science.

As a young student in college, it is only reasonable to feel apprehensive about performing poorly in classes, in the sense, we might make terrible decisions to avoid failing, but the results will make finding the life we want more challenging. However, if we adjust our attitude and begin to consider failures as stepping stones to success, we can open the way more effectively than before.

The majority of students who attend college on a limited budget are concerned that if they choose a career path solely based on their interests or if they are unable to find a job that is suitable for them shortly after graduation, they will be unable to take advantage of any opportunities in the future. Due to this, people may feel obligated to make a quick decision regarding their employment. Either they must get a job right after college, regardless of whether it is something they enjoy, or they must choose a high-paying career path to avoid being in debt for the rest of their lives. Both options are necessary to avoid becoming trapped in a cycle of debt. On the other hand, this will not result in happiness once college is over.

After completing my undergraduate degree, I was interested in pursuing a Master's in Environmental Biology as that subject fascinated me immensely. The reasons were that I used to go to river banks with my friends and look for new plant species. I also connected deeply with the environment as I used to sit alone for hours near nature, such as forest areas, ponds, lakes, and rivers. Unfortunately, T. P. College did not have an Environmental Biology specialization. Consequently, I started looking for a Master's program in Environmental Biology outside the city.

Meanwhile, I started preparing for competitive exams for government sector jobs like Public Service Commission and was also looking for Master's programs. Finally, I found a Master's program in Environmental Science at Anugrah Narayan College (A. N. C.), Patna, a public college. I applied for the program, sat for the entrance exam and interview, and qualified for admission.

I did my Master's thesis on Vermicomposting and was very passionate about it. Additionally, I thought I would advance my research in this area only. While waiting for my Master's exam result, I joined a private school as a science teacher as I wanted to be financially independent. After a few months, I was offered to teach at my host college (A. N. C.) in the Environment and Water Management department. During this period, I was also responsible for leading a team for an ambitious project sponsored by the United Nations International Children's Emergency Fund (UNICEF), the "Arsenic Project." The project was to assess groundwater arsenic contamination in Bihar. While working on this project, I encountered several incidents that motivated me to change my research area from vermicomposting to groundwater arsenic contamination. I was fully dedicated to arsenic research in the fields and laboratory during that project. My research was on and off during this period as I changed my research area, and I also did not get into any Ph.D. program; instead, I continued working as a water and sanitation professional. After completing this project, I got two job offers from UNICEF: school sanitation and arsenic mitigation. To get a diverse experience, I joined a school sanitation project. My passion for research kept reminding me to get into a Ph.D. program to continue my scientific journey. Therefore, while working on all these projects, I took pre-Ph.D. qualifying entrance exam to register for a Ph.D. program at Magadh University. I did qualify for that exam and finally got registered for my Ph.D.

2.3. First Ph.D. in India

The Ph.D. program I was registered at A. N. C., Patna did not have any course curriculum at that time. However, there is a course curriculum for Ph.D. students now. After some time, I quit my UNICEF job and started focusing on my research. Since I quit my job, I needed financial support to complete my Ph.D.. Therefore, I started looking for scholarships. I was lucky to earn a highly competitive national scholarship called the Jawaharlal Nehru Memorial Fund scholarship for my doctoral study for two years.

My Ph.D. research required field and laboratory studies. Since I had established a good relationship with the communities I worked with during "Project Arsenic," I did not have any issue conducting field studies. I was on my own in the laboratory. However, a few of my undergraduate students helped me in both fields and the laboratory. I was very passionate about my research, and I still am. Working long hours in the lab was a routine for me (Figure 1).

Figure 1. A day working in a lab in Bihar, India, in 2005.

The photograph provided here is from when I was preparing water samples for arsenic testing, which I consider one of the most beautiful pictures taken of me (Figure 2).

Figure 2. Laboratory photo of prepared water samples for arsenic testing in a lab in Bihar, India.

Adding undergraduate students to any publication was not a practice, but I believe that if a student helped in any research work, they must be either acknowledged or listed as authors based on their contribution. At that time, I broke that unethical practice in the research world, and I listed those undergraduate students as coauthors in one of my publications, where they helped me (Singh et al. 2014).

I completed my Ph.D. research and thesis writing in three years. I submitted my thesis to the University in the fourth year of my Ph.D. However, it took approximately two more years to receive the evaluation report of my Ph.D. thesis. Finally, I defended my thesis in 2012. However, at this time, I was already in the USA, in the second year of my second Ph.D.

2.4. Second Ph.D. in the US

After submitting my first Ph.D. thesis, I started looking for postdoctoral opportunities. However, I quickly realized that without good publications, support from a previous advisor, and networking among the scientific community, it is hard to get such opportunities. Unfortunately, I was out of luck with all these essential criteria. During this process, I found a good Ph.D. program in the USA. Since the Graduate Record Examination (GRE) and Test of English Foreign Language (TOEFL) were required for Ph.D. admission, I prepared for them in one month and took the exams. Although I did not score very high, I still managed to earn the score needed to get into the Ph.D. program I was interested in. Thankfully, with a full scholarship, I was accepted for the Ph.D. program in Environmental Management at Montclair State University, Montclair, New Jersey, USA.

Figure 3. A day in the laboratory in the USA in 2012.

My second Ph.D. in the USA required many courses to complete and to gain continuous financial support from the University, I had to maintain a minimum GPA. I completed all my courses on time and started my research. Once again, I selected Bihar as my project area. I did not have enough money to support my research trip and data collection. I received no support from the department except a research travel grant from the Graduate School of my University. I borrowed some money from one of my classmates, who happened to be a businessman. I did my field study in the Maner block of the Patna district of Bihar. Working in rural areas has always been a challenge in Bihar, which I have also experienced in my previous assignments. Apart from social, institutional, and political challenges, some fundamental challenges are critical such as the availability of water and food. You may find local restaurants (Dhaba) where you can hardly find good snacks (Figure 4). Therefore, I always used to keep some readymade snacks with me.

Figure 4. A local restaurant (Dhaba) in a village of Maner block of Patna District in Bihar, India, in 2013.

I am not used to carrying bottled water, so I primarily depended on hand pump water in the survey areas. It was a scorching summer when the temperature went up to 49°C. Therefore, I used to find cold water sources without arsenic for drinking (Figure 5).

Figure 5. Relaxing on nature's couch and enjoying cold water from a handpump in a village of Maner block of Patna district in Bihar, India in 2013.

I developed a good reputation with the villagers and the individuals who helped me during the survey. I never hesitated to honor their request for food at their house (Figure 6). Eating at the villagers' houses helped develop trust and a sense of belonging in the community. I found this very natural as I have always felt connected with communities, especially since I used to communicate in their local languages.

Figure 6. Lunch at a villager's house in the village of Maner block of Patna district in Bihar, India, in 2013.

The study area was flood-affected; therefore, the challenges were immense, and I had to complete my survey before the entire area got affected and there was no transportation to the villages (Figure 7).

Figure 7. The flooded area between the city and the project area in Maner block of Patna district in Bihar, India, in 2013.

I used to drive my father's van to commute from my hometown to the study area. This entire trip was perilous in various ways. For example, there was some agitation among communities about the failure of arsenic-mitigation programs in the area. Nevertheless, with the support of the villagers, I managed to complete my study in the villages.

Soon, I completed my field studies and returned to the USA to complete the data analysis and thesis preparation. Finally, I defended my Ph.D. and graduated with a good GPA (Figure 6). My dream of wearing a gown and walking on the ramp to complete the Ph.D. journey came true in 2015. In the USA, we had two ceremonies, the convocation where we received greetings from the university dean (Figure 8), the provost (Figure 9), and the president (Figure 10).

Figure 8. With the university dean on convocation day in the USA in 2015.

Figure 9. With the university provost on convocation day in the USA in 2015.

Figure 10. With the university president on convocation day in the USA in 2015.

On the commencement day, I received the honor from the college dean and the Head of the Department (Figure 11-12).

Figure 11. Ph.D. award commencement was received from the college dean and the University Department Chair at the Prudential Center, New Jersey, USA, in 2015.

Figure 12. Ph.D. award commencement was received from the college dean and the University Department Chair at the Prudential Center, New Jersey, USA, in 2015.

I cannot express my feelings when I finally graduated with a second Ph.D. degree from an American university. Unfortunately, no one from my family was there, and only a few well-wishers I met in the USA were present.

However, the journey to earn a second Ph.D. came with all possible challenges a scholar and an individual may have, except a life threat. The period between my thesis writing and graduation day was the most challenging part of my academic life. However, if I am writing this book, that means I survived the odds. More importantly, I do not want readers to get interested in the details of the challenges I faced because that may discourage them. Instead, they should find my journey as a motivation to not stop their journey towards becoming a scientist.

"There is no place on earth where you do not have challenges. Wherever humans live, there will be many challenges. Either you accept the challenge and fight back or surrender; the choice is yours."

Throughout this journey, I never abandoned my studies, gave up on my work, or stopped worshiping Goddess Saraswati. When I revisit those days, my journey reminded me of those Kashmiri Hindus who survived the world's largest genocide and became refugees in their own country but never gave up on their studies. They cannot be compared, but one common thread I found is they never gave up on earning an education and praying to Goddess Saraswati. Many of them are now leading beautiful lives. Therefore, the story's moral is that education is essential, not the challenges.

"Thousands of Kashmiri Hindus of India survived in the world's largest genocides in their own country, but they did not abandon worshiping 'Maa Saraswati.' Therefore, never get detached from books and never stop your journey to gain knowledge."

SCHOLARSHIPS

I remember my first attempt to earn a scholarship was in class seven. Somehow, I learned about that scholarship program and sat for the test without any preparation. Obviously, I could not score the qualifying marks to earn a scholarship for my studies. I wanted a scholarship because I wanted to be independent and did not want to burden my parents financially. It was just a natural feeling; there was no other reason that I should be looking for scholarships for my study. Also, wherever I went for my studies, there was no such environment where students were motivated for scholarships. However, sports, National Cadet Corps (NCC), and Scout and Guide were some of the activities where I knew that while being physically fit, we also get some advantages in our education and jobs in the future. So, I started participating in various sports activities, including 100 and 400-meter races, high jumps, long jumps, jumbling throws, and shotput ball throw. Then I joined Scout and Guide, where I achieved Governor's award. When I joined NCC during my college days, I could only reach up to B-certificate. In sports, I was good in long jump and high jump. I also led Scout and Guide team in various programs, and in NCC, I remember achieving good accuracy in shooting during an outdoor camp in the Munger district of Bihar.

After completing my Master's degree, I immediately joined a private school as a Science Teacher. Then I started teaching at a college where I also started working on a UNICEF-sponsored project, and I started earning at least to sustain myself. Later, I got a full-time position where my salary was three times the honorarium I was getting from the project. By then, the project was completed, so I accepted the full-time job offer. After 17 months, I resigned from that job and started focusing on completing my Ph.D. Unfortunately, my income ended with my resignation, and I did not want to ask for money from my parents to complete my research, so I started looking for scholarships for doctoral studies.

3.1. Jawaharlal Nehru Memorial Fund Award, India

I applied for the Jawaharlal Nehru Memorial Fund (JNMF) award for doctoral studies. The test center was in New Delhi, where several students came from all over India. I was nervous after talking to other students as they were good students. I think there were only a few scholarships available every year. However, I was selected for the interview and was pretty confident because I worked in the lab and the field to challenge myself and pursue my Ph.D. research. I still remember the well-known professor of Jawaharlal Nehru University, New Delhi, India, who interviewed me. The interview went well, and I was granted a two-year scholarship. The scholarship amount was approximately 60% of the salary I used to earn before starting my Ph.D. research. However, it was enough for me to sustain and complete my work.

The best part of the scholarship was that I used to get the fund directly to my bank account, so I never had to deal with any complicated administrative processes that many scholars suffer from.

3.2. Doctoral Assistantship, Montclair State University, New Jersey, USA

Ph.D. programs in the US were highly competitive, and I believe all of them were funded, so if a student is accepted for the program, they get scholarships; then it depends on the performance. If the performance of students is good, they could secure the scholarship for four consecutive years. The scholarship amounts vary from program to program and college to college. I got a full scholarship, including a full tuition waiver and stipend. The stipend was good enough for those who wanted to live a student life. My expenses were need-based, so I was doing well with the stipend and could save some money, thanks to my mother, who taught me the art of saving money. Almost all my classmates had a car, but I never felt the need to buy one. I commuted by public transport, which was terrific in New Jersey. As students, we used to get discounts for bus passes.

Whatever my challenges were, I ensured I was on track with my studies and did not lose my scholarship. As a result, I could continue getting a full scholarship for four years, and I completed my research work within four years.

I also earned a Student Research and Conference Fund Award for my research. During this period, I did apply for project grants but could not get additional funds. However, I applied for an international scholarship and it was about to be offered when my department's admin told me that if I took the international grant, I would lose University's scholarship, so I had to give up that opportunity.

After my second Ph.D., I started working as a Data Scientist, so the scholarship journey paused here. If I decide to study full-time in the future, I may look for possible grants and scholarships again.

ANALYTICAL AND LABORATORY TRAINING

4.1. Laboratory Skills

Although my laboratory analytical training started in my 12th grade in India and continued till my 2nd Ph.D. in the US, I remember my dissection skills were excellent as I used to efficiently dissect frogs and cockroaches and take their brain and gizzards out safely. During undergraduate studies, the majority of experiments were around dissecting plants.

I was exposed to environmental analytical instruments during my Master's education. Gradually, I was fascinated with the instruments. After graduating with a Master's in Environmental Science, I got an opportunity to work as an Adjunct Professor (resource person) at the Department of Environment and Water Management of A. N. C., Patna, Magadh University, Bihar, India. I was also in-charge of the environmental instrumentation lab.

My fascination for environmental analytical instruments went up to another level. I learned, taught, and used these instruments—Ultra Violet Spectrophotometer, Flame Photometer, pH Meter, etc.— for various projects and my Ph.D. research in India.

The laboratory was like a "Mandir (temple)" for me. I still remember when I used to clean and mop the laboratory regularly by myself. I also bought curtains for windows and covers for open racks.

The peons used to tell me, "Sir, let me do that." But I used to broom and mop the lab by myself, which gave me self-satisfaction. At this lab, I did a lot of experiments, primarily on arsenic contamination in water, soil, and plants. All instruments were well maintained and functional except a few.

Later, I got exposed to the latest analytical instruments, such as Inductively Coupled Plasma Mass Spectrophotometer, Inductively Coupled Plasma Optical Emission Spectrometry, High-performance Liquid Chromatography, Atomic Spectrophotometry, and many more cutting-edge analytical instruments during my second Ph.D. in the US. I conducted all laboratory analyses related to my scholarship and Ph.D.-related research. As I mentioned in the previous section, I was fascinated with analytical instruments. So, I learned all about advanced instruments, including their operation and troubleshooting.

I want to highlight one specialized training on Scanning Electron Microscope (SEM). The professor who used to offer a specialized course on SEM was known to be the toughest professor at the University, but she was a great scientist, and passing her course test was perceived to be a challenging goal to achieve. I wanted to learn the instrument from the best of the best and apply SEM to detect arsenic and other toxic chemicals in plants and other biological samples. I dedicated myself to the training and earned a good grade in that course.

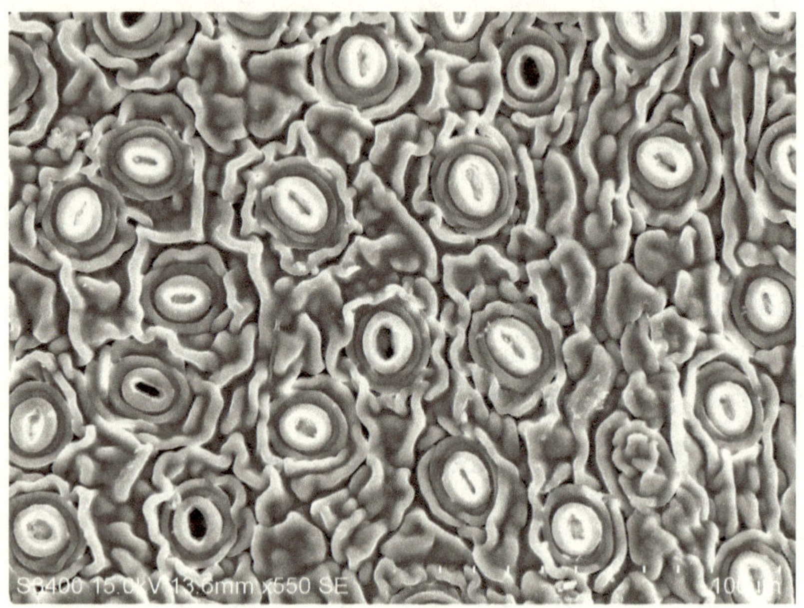

Figure 13. SEM image of a plant sample.

Although I could not use SEM further in my research, that training is still preserved in the corner of my neurons. During this period, I learned about so many other analytical instruments and methods that I could not use further in my research as I did not get any opportunities in academic or research institutions where I could continue utilizing my lab training for research activities. Therefore, all upcoming research was quantitative, where I primarily used quantitative methods, including statistics, machine learning, and geospatial tools and techniques.

4.2. Quantitative Analytical Skills

Although the concepts of statistics were introduced during my undergraduate, I did not pay much attention to those methods until I started working on my Master's thesis, followed by Ph.D. research. As I was soaked up in biology, I was not interested in mathematics or statistics during my undergraduate. During my first Ph.D., I did not know about any sophisticated statistical tools, and I could not afford the subscription to the available tools. I analyzed all my Ph.D. data in Excel Spreadsheets. I created all statistical models in the Excel spreadsheet by creating all the equations using Excel spreadsheet functions. I started getting into data analytics because I developed all the statistical models by creating those equations in an Excel spreadsheet.

During my Ph.D. in the US, I was extensively exposed to JMP and SPSS statistical analytical tools. I used both tools equally and performed all data analysis using them. I undertook several specialized statistical courses at this time. I was exposed to data mining, machine learning, cloud computing, and other advanced quantitative tools and techniques. This was the time when I was also exposed to R programming language and RStudio statistical analytical tool.

After graduation, I took specialized training on several new technologies such as artificial intelligence, data modeling, Python, Tableau, and Big Data, but I was not limited to only these. I could say that this was the phase where I was well-trained for modeling, policy creation, multidisciplinary research, and developing various prediction models.

4.3. Geospatial Skills

The story of me learning geospatial skills is fascinating. I was exposed to Geospatial techniques, such as capturing coordinates of sampling locations using the Global Positioning System (GPS), in 2004 during the UNICEF-sponsored Project Arsenic. At the time, I was also introduced to mapping tools. I quickly realized the power of those tools and eagerly started looking for opportunities to learn them. Many incidents can be cited to show my eagerness to learn the usage of those tools. However, the most prominent is when I started chasing individuals around me who knew the same. There was an opportunity when the host department could send scholars for such training, but they decided to send faculty members rather than the scholars. Until 2010 I could not succeed in this effort, but I never gave up on anything in my life, so that eagerness was always in me. When I joined another Ph.D. program at the US University, there was a well-established Geographic Information Systems Laboratory. I thought that my chase to learn geospatial tools and techniques would end here. I was fortunate because the GIS mentor I got was a genius.

I learned GIS well, and my mentor complimented me saying, "Sushant, you came to the US to learn GIS, and you made it after EIGHT long years of wait." I started utilizing what I learned about GIS in my research, upcoming publications, and even in the industry I worked with. Later, I also learned QGIS and performed Geospatial analysis in R and Python programming languages.

I consolidated all my learnings and experiences and wrote an article to guide many other students on how to shape their careers in environmental informatics or environmental data science. This publication became the most downloaded and read article of the year 2018-2019 (Singh 2019). After this publication, several students and professionals contacted me for guidance, making me feel that it was worth writing that article.

THE BEGINNING OF SCIENTIFIC THOUGHTS

*D*uring my childhood, there were several instances where I may have discovered many things or I may have created many things, but I cannot say that I was very fond of scientists. I remember my undergraduate days when I used to go for Botany tuition classes; I learned that Chlorophyll and Mitochondria were the two essential aspects of plant life. Chlorophyll is a pigment that can perform photosynthesis, making plants self-sustainable for food production. On the other hand, Mitochondria are the cell's powerhouse that supports all cell energy requirements. I was so moved that the need for food and energy would be solved if I could produce chlorophyll and mitochondria synthetically. That is what all living creatures need! I was so excited and shared the thought with my professor and friends. I think that conversation was lost somewhere. However, the scientist within me was born that day. Those days were the most memorable in my life as a student, and I learned a lot and worked extremely hard to be well-prepared for my exams.

Furthermore, the goal was to earn a gold medal at my graduation. Although I scored a good grade, I could not earn the first rank in the university. The disappointing part is that we did not have a convocation ceremony. My never-give-up attitude told me to move on. During my undergraduate studies, I searched for plants with my friends. In the laboratory, we used to do a lot of dissections. All these motivated me to learn more about environmental biology. I thought that during my Master's I would specialize in Environmental Biology. Unfortunately, we did not have any other specialization than Pathology in the college I did my undergraduate. So, I started looking outside Madhepura. I found A. N. C., Patna, where there was a Master's program in Environmental Science. I started preparing for the entrance exam. At the same time, I was also preparing for other exams to get a good job. When the day came, the entrance date for both MS and the job (Public Service Commission) collided. There was no way I could manage both exams as I had to go out of state for the PSC exam. I decided to sit for the MS entrance test exam. I cleared the test and the interview and got admitted to the MS program in Environmental Science.

This program probably helped me see data from multidisciplinary perspectives as we had to learn almost all subjects. Environmental instrumentation classes were fascinating. By now, I was mentally prepared to pursue my academic career as a faculty and scientist. My first in-depth research as a student was on vermicomposting. At the end of the project, I discovered how micro and macronutrients in the soil could be improved organically. After completing the final exams, I immediately joined a school as a science teacher. While waiting for my MS exam results, I was preparing for NET/

JRF and other research opportunities. One day I received a call with an offer to teach and take laboratory classes for undergraduate students in the Environment and Water Management program at the same college I was pursuing my Master's. I started teaching there and thought about pursuing my Ph.D. After some time, I got an opportunity from the same department to lead a UNICEF-sponsored project on groundwater arsenic contamination in Bihar. I invested my life in that project and worked in the field and lab. In this project, I got the opportunity to work with communities. My team and I physically traveled to many villages and districts to collect water samples and test them in the field and lab. This project produced much primary high-quality data. Although the project outcomes were presented at many national and international conferences, there were no peer-reviewed journal article publications. This project motivated me to switch my research interest from Vermicomposting to groundwater arsenic contamination. I took a pre-Ph.D. entrance test and succeeded in getting registered as a Ph.D. scholar in the same department. After some time, for my doctoral study, I applied for a prominent national fellowship, Jawaharlal Nehru Memorial Fellowship. I earned that fellowship by completing my Ph.D. research within the required timeline. My journey during this Ph.D. itself is an independent project to write. In short, even with all the limitations, I could submit my thesis on time. Although I had some outstanding findings from my research, I did not have any publications apart from my Ph.D. work. Without publications, I knew I would not get any academic or scientific positions in good institutions. Instead of waiting, I started applying for postdoctoral positions. I had one very promising interview of approximately two hours for a postdoctoral position at Michigan Technology University,

Michigan, USA. I did not make it, probably because the other candidate had a couple of publications. I continued my search. Until now, I have been doing science a lot, such as investigating and assessing. I wanted to work on solutions, management, modeling, and policies. An incident inspired my thought process during our fieldwork. One day, we were testing a hand pump for arsenic contamination. Unfortunately, the water had 80ppb arsenic, and we painted the hand pump's spout RED to mark it unsafe. When we finished our work, an 8-10-year-old kid started drinking water from the same hand pump. I was numbed. That day I decided to extend my research to provide solutions, not just to keep investigating and discovering environmental challenges.

I was working on publishing my research works but did not see that happening for a year or so. This way, getting a postdoctoral position at a good university was certainly not positive. While searching for academic opportunities, I found an excellent Ph.D. program in Environmental Management at Montclair State University, NJ, USA. This was not a simple path to walk on. I also needed to prepare for Graduate Record Examinations (GRE) and take up Test of English as a Foreign Language (TOEFL). Somehow, I prepared and took both tests. Though I did not score outstandingly, whatever I got secured me admission and a full scholarship for the Ph.D. program in Environmental Management at Montclair State University, NJ, USA.

When my second Ph.D. started, I met many great professors, scientists, and geniuses. I learned a lot about various research methods, laboratory instruments, analytical and geospatial techniques, and publishing in peer-reviewed journals.

THE JOURNEY AS
A SCIENTIST

While pursuing my second Ph.D., I also started focusing on publishing my first Ph.D. research work. I was on a mission to publish on my own. I submitted the first research paper to a new Indian journal because of its concise publication period. It was not a predatory journal; the publisher was reputed in India for academic publications. My first publication was based on a pot experiment on the impact of arsenic on chlorophyll content.

It is a pleasant coincidence that I wanted to synthesize chlorophyll during my undergraduate studies and I experimented with chlorophyll during my first Ph.D. research work, which became my first publication as a first author. Although the article got published in a simple journal, it was cited by many top researchers and published in good journals. My first publication was an excellent research outcome of my first Ph.D. My first Ph.D. produced a total of 4 peer-reviewed journal articles and one monograph.

After completing my second Ph.D., I started looking for academic and research positions again. However, I did not get what I sought in the US or India. Maybe there was a mismatch between what the world wanted and what I had for academic and research positions.

I was in the US and going through an economic crisis at this stage, as my fellowship ended long ago. I was somehow surviving and desperately looking for job opportunities but found nothing. One day, I saw a data scientist job position. I reviewed the job description and was surprised to learn that I had been practicing most of the skill sets required for the role for several years, except a few. I contacted the consulting firm and asked them to help me find opportunities. In a couple of months, I had three interviews, out of which I cracked two significant opportunities. And then, my journey as a data scientist began. Unlike what I wanted, it was a different world, a corporate world. After initial adjustments, I found myself the best fit for that world as the training and skillsets I learned in the past were extremely helpful.

There was a constant argument between what I wanted and what I got. One day, I thought that what I got was the dream of 100s of thousands of individuals and that I could still achieve what I wanted. Since then, the scientist within me has been working every day. I continued working, published my previous research, presented at various conferences, and collaborated with many top scientists worldwide.

I earned two Ph.D. degrees with full scholarships in nine years, one from India and one from the USA. Until today, I have published a total of 46 peer-reviewed journal articles, two books, and six book chapters. Moreover, I am on the path to earning a Doctoral degree in Business Administration from the Swiss School of Business and Management, Geneva, Switzerland, specializing in Artificial Intelligence and Data Security.

SEARCH FOR TEACHING & RESEARCH OPPORTUNITIES

When I was about to complete my Ph.D. in the US, I started looking for teaching and research positions, primarily in India. I was desperate to find a place in academia to accomplish my scientific goals and share my knowledge, skills, and experiences with students through teaching. I believe my knowledge, skills, and experiences were much needed in India for bright students lacking resources, proper guidance, and opportunities. Therefore, I wanted to reach out to several other "Sushants."

One thing I learned in my life is that you may not get what you want, so you need to start loving what you get and dedicate yourself to that because that decision was destined. Instead of blaming the situation, people, and the system, it's better to put our sincere efforts into what we have. Still, I never let the scientist inside me die.

I got a great opportunity in the industry as a data scientist where I utilized all my skills, knowledge, and experiences and have been very successful so far. I also enjoy what I do as my profession. While working in the corporate industry, I continued my teaching and research through collaborations. I graduated in 2015, and till then, I was able to publish 12 peer-reviewed research articles. And between 2015 and 2022, I published 36 peer-reviewed research articles, books, and chapters with high-impact publishing houses.

7.1. Applications for Paid Faculty Positions

When I started applying for faculty positions in India, I primarily targeted growing universities or colleges. Therefore, all central universities and the Indian Institute of Technology institutions were out of my list. I applied to almost 40 Indian universities, institutions, and colleges for Assistant Professor positions. In most of the cases, I did not even receive any acknowledgment, and rest of the cases, I was not eligible for the position. I could not figure out what was happening and why I was not getting a response back. I did have one interview at a budding university, and it went well. Only the salary and other benefits, such as health and housing were supposed to be negotiated. Unfortunately, I did not get any teaching positions. By now, I had started figuring out what must be the reasons. I invested much time reviewing universities and college websites about existing faculty profiles to understand what the institution looks for in faculty. When I started comparing my academic and research profiles with those faculty members, it was surprising that I had better academic, research, and industry experiences in almost all cases.

Moreover, I had more research publications than many existing faculty members. What I was lacking was a reference from any bigshot in India. Many arsenic scientists in India and abroad knew me very well, but I could not ask them to write a recommendation letter for me. My referees were renowned scientists in their field but were in foreign countries, such as the USA and Australia. The result of this effort was that a candidate with two Ph.D. degrees, one from India and another from the US, with full scholarships and several publications, did not get any teaching position in Indian Universities. I could only assume why it happened, but concluding based on assumptions is not a good idea. Under all such situations, I only think that I have a different destiny written for me. I spent a reasonable amount of time trying to find an answer to this question and I realized that it is not what we want that is the best for us; what we are given is much better than what we could imagine. Consequently, I moved on to a dream job many would aspire for at that time and even now. However, I continued teaching wherever I could and published my research works.

7.2. Application for Voluntary Teaching Positions

Since I got a job and became financially independent, I have never charged any fee for teaching or lectures. There was a period when I started approaching several colleges in Bihar, other Indian states, and many South African countries. I offered free teaching and guidance to students. However, I quickly realized that free teaching is more expensive than paid teaching. I think nobody wanted any free service. This was a time I was also debating whether the education system is globally more or less the same. However, I cannot conclude anything because I do not have any concrete evidence. As a result, I stopped approaching any institutions.

7.3. Application for Faculty Position in Bihar

I graduated with a Master's in Environmental Science from A. N. C., Patna. The Environmental Science Department was established in 1988. Furthermore, there has been no faculty recruitment to teach Environmental Science since then. Professors from various science and arts streams taught all the environmental science classes. I graduated in 2003 and until then, the situation was the same. Several of my seniors also tried raising this issue and demanded the recruitment of environmental science graduates to teach Environmental Science. However, nothing happened. I also initiated an extensive campaign with my colleagues to include Environmental Science as an independent subject and hire Environmental Science graduates to teach it. We wrote about this to the then Chief Minister and the Honorable Governor of Bihar. However, nothing happened. In 2020, the state recruiting agency of Bihar published an Environmental Science assistant professor recruitment notification. I thought, at least now things will change.

At that time, I was in the USA. I applied for the position online and mailed the application to the concerned authority. However, I did not receive any acknowledgment of my application. Unfortunately, nothing happened for two years because of the COVID-19 pandemic and delays from the agency. In 2022, a notification was issued for acceptance and rejection of applications.

My application was on the list of 'ineligibles' because they did not receive the hard copy of the application I mailed. I did not have any proof that I mailed as many documents were displaced during relocation from the USA to India. However, I did have proof that I submitted my application online and successfully paid the application fees. Fortunately, I was visiting my family in Patna, so I decided to investigate what had happened. The reasons for meeting the authority to understand why my application was declared 'ineligible' and what opportunities I may have to qualify for the interview was not my application; instead, I wanted to fight for many other applicants whose application was also rejected for the same reason. I intended that if an online application is submitted along with the application fee, the job applicants should be allowed to attend an interview or have the opportunity to submit the hard copy of the application because no applicants received any notification of receiving their applications by the agency. I went to the authority to discuss my issue. At first, I was outrightly told that nothing could be done, but when I explained my situation, I was asked to come after a week. After a week, I went to meet the authority, but he was not in the office, so I kept waiting for six hours, but he did not show up.

Additionally, no office member has any information on whether he will come to the office or not. I had no other option but to contact the Governor's office to inform them about the situation and seek their help. When I called the Governor's office, I was advised to submit an e-mail or hardcopy application to schedule a meeting with the Honorable Governor. I sent an e-mail to the Governor's office explaining the entire issue. Since then, I had not received any response. I recently learned that the entire recruitment process was jeopardized because of a court case in the Patna high court. The high court stated that the recruitment process was "unlawful and in complete violation of the applicable rules of reservations as mandated by the Constitution of India[1]."

This is not the first time such an incident had occurred in Bihar. But, as Bihari (a native of Bihar), we are all aware of this and mentally prepared for such circumstances.

Furthermore, this situation suggests that faculty recruitment is not an academic affair but an administrative, personal, and political affair. In three decades, nothing has changed but has somewhat degraded. Many private universities have mushroomed in Bihar, growing very fast. Similar to how government schools were destroyed and private institutions flourished, government colleges will sink and private universities and colleges will bloom. Whether this is a systematic approach to destroying the education system of Bihar requires a forensic investigation.

---

[1]https://www.livelaw.in/news-updates/patna-high-court-bihar-state-university-service-commission-recruitment-assistant-professor-reservation-backlog-vacancy-223026

THE
COLLABORATORS

*F*rom a theoretical point of view, concerns have been raised regarding authorial collaboration projects. Academics are interested in developing methods that will allow them to determine who is responsible for what and whose ideas belong to whom. In particular, collaborative authorship within the scientific community has historically been looked down upon in favor of individual authors. In these situations, the way academics think about problems like attribution and tenure is influenced by outdated notions of individual geniuses. Nevertheless, despite the concerns and uncertainties, I have, during my career, successfully collaborated with others on a large number of projects.

As a Ph.D. scholar, I used to think I was the sole person responsible for designing and conducting my research, analyzing the data, writing a thesis, transforming research outcomes into research articles, presenting them at conferences, and publishing them in peer-reviewed journals. This was the sole reason I learned everything needed to complete my Ph.D. research successfully.

However, it is a challenging task to master all the required skills, especially when your research is multidisciplinary. At the beginning of my publication days, most of my research articles were from my first Ph.D., where I did everything by myself. Some of my research articles may not fall under a very high level of writing samples; however, all were based on lab-based findings. Gradually, I learned scientific writing and kept improving my scientific writing skills.

Soon, I realized that research publication is a full-grown industry where outsiders don't know what is happening inside. I started observing that several publications with average content were published in high-impact journals, and in these publications, either big research groups were involved or famous scientists. No doubt that this is not a general statement, but they were apparent. My research ethics never provoked me to invite "ghost authors." Therefore, to collaborate, I needed to expand my work to collaborate on those aspects—for example, applying artificial intelligence and machine learning to my research— where I may need support.

As I always say, "Where there is a will there is a way." It felt like a miracle when I saw the legendary scientist Late Dr. Dipankar Chakraborti's email in my inbox. In his email, he appreciated my research and recommended that I collaborate with others. I agreed with his advice and showed my willingness to work with him. He was too kind to let me work with him. I was able to publish two research articles with him. After getting to know him, I started admiring him more and more. It felt like the kind of scientist I was looking for was him—a brilliant scientist and a rare human being in this Kaliyuga (the age of darkness when spirituality is eclipsed by selfishness and dogmatic materialism[2]). He devoted his entire

---

[2] https://popularvedicscience.com/history/yugas/kali-yuga/

life to arsenic and fluoride research and affected communities. We were working on our third paper for the Environmental Health Perspective journal; however, we could not complete it as he passed away. He is still my role model as a scientist. The immense pain is that I could never meet him; we had conversations only a few times and apart from that we used to communicate through e-mails.

Another legendary scientist I collaborated with is Dr. Biswajeet Pradhan, a brilliant and fabulous human being. I found him on ResearchGate while looking for a collaborator for my upcoming multidisciplinary publications, where I have used machine learning to develop various prediction models. Dr. Pradhan is among the world's top scientists in the machine learning space. I was delighted when he agreed to collaborate with me. I learned a lot from him. Moreover, I was able to produce high-quality publications in our collaboration.

The collaboration journey continued, and I was able to work with an influential research group of machine learning scientists with whom I published several excellent research articles.

Collaboration is beneficial when the research is interdisciplinary so that all scientists can contribute equally and provide different perspectives. However, one can use collaboration to become a publication machine, which is neither healthy for scientists nor society.

I am willing to collaborate with anthropologists and psychologists to advance my research and address some of anthropology and psychology's less-explored theories and hypotheses.
The following section summarizes my scholarly contributions so far.

9

SCHOLARLY CONTRIBUTIONS

*T*hrough scholarly contributions, scientists advance science; this is one of the most important responsibilities of scientists. I was unaware of the research publication world until I joined my Master's program. However, we did not have any classes on scientific writing. Some of my seniors used to write in daily newspapers, and later I learned that a scientist should present their work through peer-reviewed publications. I still remember writing about various environmental issues, such as the impact of dioxins on human potency, how plants help reduce soil erosion in river catchment areas, and many more. Because of my lack of knowledge and awareness about scholarly publications, I could not publish them initially. Later, all my publications were based on in-depth research on existing literature. One consistent practice has been to never stop writing and never discarding them; most of them are still in my old files.

"Never dump your ideas; let it go to the scientific community and let them review and provide feedback, even after decades of the inception of your ideas, publish them."

The following section summarizes my publications till 2022 in chronological order.

9.1. Effect of Arsenic on Photosynthesis, Growth, and its Accumulation in the Tissues of Allium cepa (Onion)

This research article resulted from my first Ph.D. as the first author. As I mentioned in the previous sections, my first research idea was to synthesize chlorophyll and mitochondria artificially, and consequently, my first publication was also on chlorophyll. Although this article was published in an elementary journal, it received high traction among scientific communities and has been cited by many good scientists published in highly reputed journals. This paper made me realize that good quality work gets recognition (Singh and Ghosh 2010). However, this research needed further investigation and I am glad that many papers that cited my work have tried to fill the research gaps.

9.2. Entry of Arsenic into Food Material–A Case Study

This research pioneered the findings of arsenic contamination in the food chain in Bihar, India (Singh and Ghosh 2011). Arsenic concentrations were detected in wheat, maize, rice grain, rice husks, and lentils. This was a pioneering work in the Bihar state. This research further helped the department secure good grants from government agencies. To advance this research, I have several research hypotheses on my wish list that I would like to test either by myself or with the help of my students if I get any opportunities. Unfortunately, after almost 11 years, I still do not see much progress on this topic.

9.3. Arsenic Contamination in Water, Soil, and Food Materials in Bihar

This is the first Ph.D. thesis published as a monograph (Singh 2011). I wanted the monograph to be made at a lower price, but the publisher set the price based on the market value. However, most of the works have already been published as research articles. However, there are some findings still buried in the monograph. For example, one of the minor objectives I did not publish as a research article was chromosomal aberration due to arsenic. My laboratory experiments could have been advanced; however, I did not observe much advancement in this direction yet.

9.4. Health Risk Assessment Due to Groundwater Arsenic Contamination: Children Are at High Risk

This research article was from my first Ph.D. that produced an arsenic health-risk model, the first health-risk model in the region (Singh and Ghosh 2012). The arsenic health-risk models were created for children, adults, and older people. The study collected information about arsenicosis patients, and their actual consumption of water and food, which helped develop a health risk model based on field data.

9.5. Groundwater Arsenic Contamination and Associated Health Risks in Bihar, India

This research article was another outcome of my first Ph.D., where I developed an arsenic health-risk model in two districts of Bihar (Singh et al. 2014).

9.6. Multiple Groundwater Contaminations in the Mid-Gangetic Plain, Bihar (India): A Potential Threat

This study was one of the essential publications proposing a new hypothesis of how multiple groundwater contaminations could add to an individual's health issues (Singh, Sanchez, and Panigrahi 2014). For this paper, I collaborated with two scientists. Although the journal was not a mainstream journal, I wanted to let my idea go to scientific communities and let them evaluate it. I believe a cocktail of contaminants, such as arsenic, fluoride, and nitrate, can adversely impact human health, and treating the symptoms would be highly challenging. The maximum contamination levels in such environments should be regulated, especially in rural areas where the exposed population lives under deprived resources.

9.7. Disaster Issues and Management in Farm and Urban Crop Production

While pursuing my second Ph.D. in the USA, I established good collaborations with some of the great scientists on campus. This publication was a commentary paper based on our collaborative research (Singh, Feldman, and Wunderlich 2014a, b). This commentary paper highlights the need for a policy for community gardens developed in contaminated areas.

9.8. Heavy Metal Contamination Levels in Vegetables Grown in an Urban Community Garden in the Northeast USA: A Preliminary Study

The previous commentary was based on this collaborative research at MSU (Singh, Feldman, and Wunderlich 2014b). This research paper evaluated the soil of the community gardens and the plants grown in it for various contaminations.

9.9. Mapping Composite Vulnerability to Groundwater Arsenic Contamination: An Analytical Framework and a Case Study in India

I would consider this research article as the first publication from my second Ph.D. research work, and a very significant one (Singh and Vedwan 2015). This paper is based on a method I developed to quantify composite vulnerability indices and has an interesting story. After many hiccups initially, when I started submitting my works to journals for publication, it got rejected as quickly as possible, and it appeared as if someone was waiting for the article to enter the editorial system. Finally, the paper was published, and many scientists appreciated the method. In recent times, I have modified the method to make it more comprehensive. I may publish an updated version of the method soon. I also created an R-package of the method to make other scientists' life easy. However, I have not been able to publish it yet.

9.10. Assessing and Mapping Vulnerability and Risk Perceptions to Groundwater Arsenic Contamination: Towards Developing Sustainable Arsenic Mitigation Models

This is the Ph.D. thesis published as a part of the University's requirement (Singh 2015b). My research was multidisciplinary and the study had several novel elements. One of the study's objectives was to perceive people's risk and its role in adopting arsenic-mitigation technologies. This research was also featured in Nature Asia journal (Priyadarshini 2014).

9.11. Groundwater Arsenic Contamination in the Middle-Gangetic Plain, Bihar (India): The Danger Arrived

This is another independent but significant research article (Singh 2015a). Humans tend to not learn from past mistakes and repeat them. This publication highlights how the dangers of arsenic were raised in 2003, and the research group warned the scientific community and policy-makers about the impending danger in the state of Bihar (Chakraborti et al. 2003). This article also highlights the challenge of "elite capture" in scientific investigations. It can be considered as raising practical challenges in the research world that impact science and society by not doing the right thing at the right time.

9.12. Paleoenvironmental Evidence for the First Human Colonization of the Eastern Caribbean

As mentioned in the previous section, I had the opportunity to collaborate with many great scientists at MSU, a group of the world's great anthropologists provided me with the opportunity to work with them on their very ambitious project on paleoenvironmental studies in the Eastern Caribbean (Siegel et al. 2015). This was a great learning experience where I met brilliant but very humble scientists. I also learned that accepting and rejecting original research work is part of the publication process in peer-reviewed journals.

"However, later, I thought about what makes journals' editors or reviewers better scientists than senior and well-established scientists who document their scientific investigation based on actual field and laboratory experiments. I still do not have a satisfactory answer to this question."

9.13. Evaluating Hydrogeological and Topographic Controls on Groundwater Arsenic Contamination in the Middle-Ganga Plain in India: Towards Developing Sustainable Arsenic Mitigation Models

This book chapter was based on an in-depth investigation of geospatial data, including hydrogeological and topographic factors in the arsenic-contaminated area. The study provided evidence of elevated arsenic levels close to the River Ganga and suggested that River Sone alluvium could be a potential source of arsenic contamination in Bihar, India (Singh, Brachfeld, and Taylor 2016). In addition, several new predictors of arsenic contamination that could be used to develop regional arsenic prediction models were identified. Although I did develop a methodological framework of arsenic prediction (unpublished), I did not get the opportunity to complete it. However, there are several articles on arsenic prediction or other contaminants, such as fluoride and nitrate. However, I still believe there is a need for a regional prediction model because global models may not be accurate and applicable to local topographic and hydrogeological conditions. I hope some well-established research groups will develop such models or new generation scientists may take the lead on this work.

9.14. Geospatial Analysis of Census Data for Targeting New Businesses Using Geoeconomics

In the training section of this book, you will find a paragraph where I have mentioned that I have attempted to use my learnings in the industry I worked in. This publication was motivated by how academic training can be utilized to achieve industries' goals. This research article provides an in-depth analysis of how open data, i.e., US census data, can help in critical decision-making using geospatial tools and techniques (Singh 2016). The US Census data is rich and accurate; it can help in several ways and in all domains. Wherever I have worked, I have always attempted to introduce the advantage of US Census data and geospatial tools and techniques.

9.15. Conceptual Framework for a Cloud-based Decision Support System For Arsenic Health Risk Assessment

This paper is one of my dream projects I still want to implement (Singh 2017b). After the article's publication, I contacted several research groups but did not receive a positive response. Later, I decided to implement it by myself whenever time and resources permitted. I am hoping to pick this work up in 2023 and complete it.

9.16. Arsenic: Occurrence in Groundwater

This encyclopedia entry is one of the most important publications (Chakraborti et al. 2011). Late Dr. Dipankar Chakraborti, a legendary scientist who extensively worked on arsenic and fluoride issues, contacted me to appreciate my research publications. I felt fortunate to have had that experience. Although I was working in the industry, I expressed my interest in working with him on any of his ongoing projects so that I could learn from him. He obliged and offered the opportunity to work on updating his original encyclopedia article on arsenic. I did not expect to be a co-author for this work, as the opportunity to learn from him was more remarkable than a publication.

When we completed the work, he made me the second author of this article and said, "You have earned it." I could only express my gratitude to him. He was a true scientist; he still is for me. I see myself growing older like him and leaving a legacy to be followed by other scientists.

9.17. Global Arsenic Contamination: Living with the Poison Nectar

The co-author of this commentary article is a genius of environmental management. I requested him to collaborate on writing a commentary on global arsenic contamination (Singh and Stern 2017). We worked together, and the commentary was accepted quickly for publication. Collaboration is another way of learning from great scientists and professionals. The co-author is the best blend of academia and industry, and I hope to continue learning from and working with him.

9.18. Evaluating Two Freely Available Geocoding Tools for Geographical Inconsistencies and Geocoding Errors

This publication was industry-centric (Singh 2017c). While using various geocoding techniques, I realized some discrepancies in some existing methods. Therefore, I worked on this article to highlight those gaps. Sometimes, your work triggers new paths for many scientists or professionals. I did observe that several studies were conducted based on a similar theme to this paper. As a result, error-free geocoding improved, and I believe all such scientists contributed a lot to make it happen.

9.19. Developing Sustainable Models of Arsenic Mitigation Technologies in the Middle-Ganga Plain in India

This research article was an essential piece of work as I presented various socioeconomic arsenic-mitigation models, probably for the first time in the context of arsenic (Singh, Taylor, and Su

2017). I submitted this to India's top scientific journal. Although my paper got accepted, it took almost two years to see it in print. My biggest disappointment with this publication is it has less outreach to scientific communities, reflecting how less this article was cited. There could be several reasons for its less outreach, so nothing can be concluded confidently.

9.20. An Analysis of the Cost-effectiveness of Arsenic Mitigation Technologies: Implications for Public Policy

This is another independent research article covering arsenic mitigation policies' economic aspects (Singh 2017a). Unfortunately, only a few studies are available on the cost-effective analysis of arsenic mitigation technologies. Therefore, estimating the health benefits of interventions where the governments provide mitigation technologies is crucial. Such analyses help us adapt mitigation policies to make them sustainable from technology and socioeconomic perspectives.

9.21. A Novel Hybrid Approach of Landslide Susceptibility Modeling Using Rotation Forest Ensemble and Different Base Classifiers

I established collaboration with a prominent machine learning research scientists' group, and this piece of research was one of several publications with this research group. In this study, we developed hybrid machine-learning models to classify landslides (Thai Pham et al. 2018). I find myself fortunate to get connected with this research group, where I learned a lot as well as produced several high-quality publications.

9.22. Groundwater Arsenic Contamination in the Ganga River Basin: A Future Health Danger

This was the second and the last publication in collaboration with the late Dr. Dipankar Chakraborti. This article is one of the most highly cited papers among my other publications (Chakraborti et al. 2018). 19 years ago, Dr. Dipankar Chakraborti's team warned the world about the danger of arsenic in the future (Chakraborti et al. 2003). Post 2003, multiple research works have been done; however, the solution is still not yet obtained.

"It has been more than a century of arsenic research, billions of dollars must have been spent by research funding agencies on arsenic mitigation technologies, and thousands of Ph.D. scholars have defended their thesis on arsenic research, including me. However, we still cannot say we have solved arsenic challenges. All such situations bother me and make me think about the end goal of scientists or scientific investigations."

9.23. Developing Robust Arsenic Awareness Prediction Models Using Machine Learning Algorithms

To expand my research, I decided to apply cutting-edge artificial intelligence techniques to my current work, primarily on my 2nd Ph.D. data. Although, as I have mentioned in the collaborators' section, I was able to collaborate with Dr. Pradhan, this article was an outcome of a great collaboration with him and one of the most renowned scientists in the arsenic field, Dr. Mahmud Rahman. This study pioneered the application of various machine learning methods to classify arsenic awareness for decision-making. In addition, it also helped understand that socioeconomic and environmental data require non-linear classification algorithms to capture the inherent pattern in the data better (Singh et al. 2018).

9.24. Humanizing the Landscapes of the Lesser Antilles During the Archaic Age

This book chapter was the second publication with the paleoenvironmental scientists I worked with (Siegel et al. 2018).

9.25. Landslide Susceptibility Assessment by Novel Hybrid Machine Learning Algorithms

This research article was another outcome in collaboration with machine-learning scientists, where we produced hybrid machine-learning models to classify landslides in the Pithoragarh district of Uttarakhand in India (Pham, Prakash, et al. 2019).

9.26. Assessing the Role of Risk Perception in Ensuring Sustainable Arsenic Mitigation

This research article has an exciting story that readers should know (Singh and Taylor 2019). It was first featured in Nature Asia (Priyadarshini 2014). The first version of this article was submitted to a very reputable journal. The editor liked the work and forwarded the manuscript for review. The editor requested at least six reviewers to review the manuscript; however, all of them denied saying they did not have the expertise to do justice to the paper. The editor got disappointed, and unfortunately, he had to reject the paper. I was hopeless about where I should submit the paper. Thankfully, later I found an excellent interdisciplinary journal where I finally submitted with the hope that the editor would find suitable reviewers. I got lucky this time and finally, the paper was accepted for publication.

9.27. Assessing and Mapping Human Health Risks Due to Arsenic and Socioeconomic Correlates for Proactive Arsenic Mitigation

This book chapter is another work from my 2nd Ph.D. (<u>Singh and Taylor 2020</u>). It provides a good summary of socioeconomic and health predictors of communities living in arsenic-contaminated areas. Next-generation scientists can take these predictors and further test other hypotheses and can develop a new theory that can help develop meaningful and robust socioeconomic models of arsenic mitigation.

9.28. Landslide Susceptibility Modeling Using Reduced Error Pruning Trees and Different Ensemble Techniques: Hybrid Machine Learning Approaches

This work is another good collaborative outcome where we attempted to develop hybrid machine learning models by combining reduced error pruning trees and various ensemble techniques (<u>Pham, Prakash, et al. 2019</u>).

9.29. Hybrid Computational Intelligence Models for Groundwater Potential Mapping

Predicting potential groundwater areas is challenging. However, in this collaborative work, we developed hybrid machine-learning models for the Vadodara district of Gujarat in India (Pham, Jaafari, et al. 2019).

9.30. Arsenic Water Resources Contamination: Challenges and Solutions

This is my first edited book where I collaborated with a great scientist and brought several other scientists worldwide to share their research as chapters (Fares and Singh 2020). It was a great learning experience to approach the right researchers and invite them to contribute to the book. And also, review and edit the work and ensure all chapters meet the publishing standard. It took almost one year to complete this journey. The book could be a good reference for environmental and sustainability scientists, professionals, students, and policymakers.

9.31. A Hybrid Intelligence Approach to Enhance the Prediction Accuracy of Local Scour Depth at Complex Bridge Piers

This work was another interesting collaborative outcome where we developed various hybrid machine-learning models for accurately predicting the local scour depth at complex piers (Tien Bui et al. 2020).

9.32. Shallow Landslide Susceptibility Mapping: A Comparison between Logistic Model Tree, Logistic Regression, Naïve Bayes Tree, Artificial Neural Network, and Support Vector Machine Algorithms

In this collaborative research, we compared several artificial intelligence methods to correctly classify shallow landslides for Bijar City in the Kurdistan province of Iran (Nhu, Shirzadi, et al. 2020).

9.33. Comparison of Support Vector Machine, Bayesian Logistic Regression, and Alternating Decision Tree Algorithms for Shallow Landslide Susceptibility Mapping Along a Mountainous Road in the West of Iran

In this collaborative study, we identified the most suitable shallow landslide classification models along the mountainous road of the Salavat Abad Saddle, Kurdistan province, Iran, by comparing three machine learning algorithms (Nhu, Zandi, et al. 2020).

9.34. Improving Voting Feature Intervals for Spatial Prediction of Landslides

In this collaborative work, our approach was to improve the performance of the voting feature intervals machine learning algorithm for landslide classification using the Muong Lay district of Vietnam as a case study (Pham, Phong, et al. 2020).

9.35. COVID-19: A Master Stroke of Nature

The COVID-19 pandemic has devasted the world by killing millions of people globally. The pandemic was also used as an opportunity by various scientists to investigate existing data and provide scientific evidence to help reduce the risks of COVID-19 infections. I intended to address some practical challenges and hypotheses I experienced and observed very closely. This piece of work provides a human behavior perspective of how unsustainable behaviors triggered this global pandemic and explains why humans must practice sustainability principles (Singh 2020). Although this article was published in a comparatively new journal, it drew the attention of various scientists who cited it in their studies.

9.36. Ensemble Modeling of Landslide Susceptibility Using Random Subspace Learner and Different Decision Tree Classifiers

In another collaborative study, we developed several ensemble machine-learning classification models for landslides in the Van Chan district of the Yen Bai Province of Vietnam (Pham et al. 2022).

9.37. A Novel Hybrid Approach of Landslide Susceptibility Modeling Using Rotation Forest Ensemble and Different Base Classifiers

This collaborative research article presents several hybrid machine-learning models for accurately classifying landslides (Pham, Prakash, et al. 2020).

9.38. Using Artificial Neural Network (ANN) for the Prediction of Soil Coefficient of Consolidation

Primarily, my research has been around environmental challenges, including groundwater contamination and natural hazards. However, this study was to help the construction engineering domain by predicting the soil coefficient of consolidation. In this collaborative research, we developed an Artificial Neural Network prediction model (Pham, Singh, and Ly 2020).

9.39. GIS-based Ensemble Soft Computing Models for Landslide Susceptibility Mapping

As I mentioned in this book's training section, I had a deep interest in geospatial tools and technologies; I got the opportunity to work on interesting collaborative research studies where we applied GIS and machine learning techniques. In this research, we developed a novel approach to improve the credal decision tree performance by using various ensemble methods for landslide susceptibility mapping in the Muong Lay district of Vietnam (Pham, Van Phong, et al. 2020).

9.40. Application of Artificial Intelligence in Predicting Groundwater Contaminants

This book chapter was intended to review various artificial intelligence techniques in developing groundwater contaminants so that the next generation of scientists can pick up some ideas and take science further (Singh, Shirzadi, and Pham 2021).

9.41. Landslide Susceptibility Modeling Using Different Artificial Intelligence Methods: A Case Study at Muong Lay District, Vietnam

This research was another collaborative work to develop landslide prediction models in the Muong Lay District of Vietnam (Phong et al. 2021).

9.42. Evaluating and Predicting Social Behavior of Arsenic Affected Communities: Towards Developing an Arsenic Resilient Society

This piece of research was from my second Ph.D. that I had been planning for a long time (Singh, Taylor, and Thadaboina 2022). Predicting social behaviors is not easy and attempting to do that as a scientific contribution is another big challenge. It took some time to conceptualize this paper; I carefully designed and started working on it. Thankfully, this paper got accepted in an excellent and high-impact journal.

9.43. Application of Novel Hybrid Machine Learning Algorithm in Shallow Landslide Susceptibility Mapping in a Mountain Area

This is another collaborative research on landslide prediction using various machine learning models in a mountainous area near the city of Kamyaran, Kurdistan province, Iran (Ghasemian et al. 2022).

9.44. Ensemble Modeling of Landslide Susceptibility Using Random Subspace Learner and Different Decision Tree Classifiers

In this collaborative study, we developed ensemble predictive machine learning models for the landslide susceptibility mapping of the Van Chan district of the Yen Bai Province, Vietnam (Pham et al. 2022).

9.45. Predicting Sustainable Arsenic Mitigation Using Machine Learning Techniques

This research article is from the second Ph.D. that I conceptualized long ago. During conceptualization, I realized that the work is complicated and should be presented in a way that readers can easily understand. Therefore, I collaborated with great machine learning scientists. Thankfully, this paper got accepted into one of the top journals in the environmental toxicology field. This study suggests that the Gaussian Naïve Bayes algorithm can understate the complex relationships of socio-environmental data, which is critical for developing robust classification models (Singh et al. 2022).

9.46. Towards Robust Smart Data-Driven Soil Erodibility Index Prediction Under Different Scenarios

This is another collaborative research where we developed machine learning prediction models for soil erodibility index for areas of Iran with soil erosion (Shirzadi et al. 2022).

9.47. Influence of Differential Arsenic Exposure on Cellular Redox Homeostasis of Exposed Rural Women of West Bengal

This is another essential piece of collaborated research I established recently. Considering the complexity of the data, it took a while for me to do justice to the data analysis. Arsenic research has been the primary focus of my research investigations and publications, as my Ph.D. studies have been related to arsenic challenges. This study is based on patient data collected from their laboratory test results (Prasad et al. 2022). Our collaboration has continued, and we look forward to more high-quality publications.

10

AWARDS, HONORS, AND RECOGNITIONS

*A*wards and honors are not what I have worked for. Most of the awards I received came to me as invitations, and I accepted them humbly. I may not remember all the awards or honors I received before my undergraduate studies as either I was unaware of all these things or we did not have such a mindset or means at home that we document everything we accomplished. Our family setting has been like that; we should not discuss our accomplishments as they may be perceived as arrogance or we might start nurturing a sense of ego. Our philosophy has been that if we do good work, it will be acknowledged sooner or later. As a result, only a few people from my family, extended family, and society who are close to me know about some of my accomplishments.

I am listing some of the awards I have received recently. However, I would like to share one event where I presented one of my research projects that the judges selected for the best presentation award. In the same event for junior sections, one of my students also got the best presentation award. However, the organizers came to me and told me that if we awarded you, then people would think that all awards went to a single institution. I smiled and said that they should do whatever they think is the right thing and that I would not have any issues. Unfortunately, the award was given to someone else. I am documenting this here not because I was hurt but because people should know there are things they read in papers or in media that happen in real life. Another incident is when I was approached by an organization for an award based on my recent work at that time; however, I was asked money and hence, I did not accept it.

10.1. First Prize in Calligraphy

I was one of the Indian representatives at the "Asian Forum for Cross-Cultural Dialogue" at Beijing University, China, in 2009. We visited the Department of Calligraphy, China Academy of Art, Hangzhou, China. We all became participants in an on-spot competition in calligraphy. Although I painted occasionally as a hobby, I never did calligraphy. Therefore, I picked the theme I used to do during my childhood. Surprisingly, the organizer picked my calligraphy as the best and awarded me the first prize (Figure 14).

Figure 14. First prize in Calligraphy in China in 2009.

10.2. Award of Honor

I was invited to the 4th International Student's Peace Festival, Chandigarh, India as a state representative for the work I have been doing in the water resources management space. It was a pleasant surprise to meet a well-known environmentalist Mr. Sundarlal Bahuguna during that event. Along with other delegates I also received an award of honor (Figure 15-16).

Figure 15. Award of honor for contributions to water resources management work, Chandigarh, India, in 2009.

Figure 16. Award of an honor group photo in Chandigarh, India, in 2009.

10.3. Alpha Epsilon Lambda (AEL)

The Alpha Epsilon Lambda Honor Society selected me based on my academic performance in my doctoral studies at Montclair State University, NJ, USA, in 2011 (Figure 17). This was probably the first award I received in the USA after joining the second Ph.D. program.

Figure 17. Alpha Epsilon Lambda induction at Montclair State University, NJ, USA, in 2011.

10.4. Student Research and Conference Fund Award

I was granted a student research and conference fund award to cover my Ph.D. research activity by the Graduate Student Organization, Montclair State University, in 2013. Although the amount is not enormous, it helped me as I did not have enough funds to travel to India for my project work, conduct surveys, collect water samples, and analyze them.

10.5. Top Downloaded Paper

I foresee several things, and one of my publications was inspired by that vision when I realized that environmental informatics or environmental data science would become a well-grown field and that many scholars with an environmental science background would get good opportunities in the industry. Therefore, I wrote an article targeting all those students and scholars who needed guidance to find good opportunities in the industry. The editor liked the paper, and after a few reviews, it was published in a top journal, Frontiers in Ecology and the Environment (Figure 18).

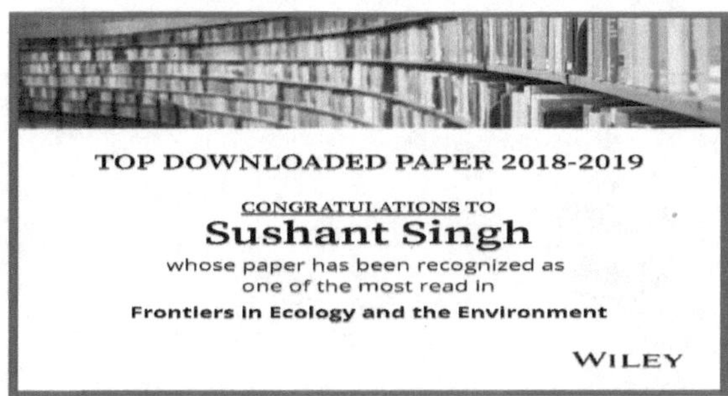

Figure 18. Top downloaded paper of 2018-2019.

Getting published in the world's top journal was a significant accomplishment, but one more piece of good news awaited me. One day I received an e-mail that my article was the most-read paper in that journal. I certainly did not expect this; however, it boosted my confidence to continue what I was doing.

10.6. Inspirational Leadership Award

I have observed that I have been approached by several agencies and institutions that honor scientists and professionals for their contributions. In such requests, I used to receive invitation e-mails to submit applications for the award category that I was either provisionally selected for or the category I found best suited to my research contributions. I did encounter one such case where the request was suspicious and potentially a fraud that I did not pursue further. In 2022, I received an Inspirational Leadership Award from Bestow Edutrex International Mumbai, India, and this award was based on my contributions to both research and the industry (Figure 19).

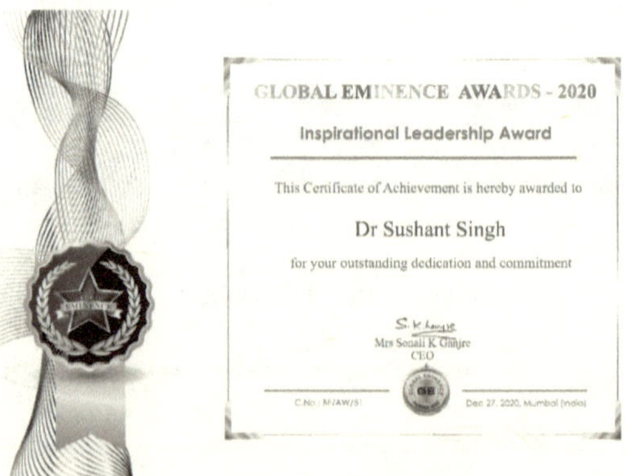

Figure 19. Inspirational leadership award in 2020.

10.7. Award for Excellence in IT

I moved to India in 2021, thinking that I would settle in India, stay with my parents, and take care of them. Therefore, I transferred from the USA to India but stayed in the same company. After a couple of months, I was approached by two reputable organizations, Indian Achievers' Forum & CSR Times to file a nomination for an award in a suitable category. Considering my current profile and previous contributions to the Information Technology industry, they honored me with an IT excellence award (Figure 20).

Figure 20. Award for excellence in IT in 2021.

10.8. Best Researcher Award

It was another surprise to me when a very reputable group approached me to submit my nomination for a suitable category for research. After reviewing my profile, they honored me with the best researcher award for my contributions and honorable achievements in innovative research by ScienceFather, India, in 2022 (Figure 21).

Figure 21. Best Researcher Award in 2022.

Indeed, all the awards I have received are not from the top-rated agencies among academics. However, had I been working in academia, I would have done more and might be eligible for some of the reputed national and international awards for scientists. Although I never worked to earn any recognition or promotion, I always respected whatever I was given, whether it be an award or a promotion. This may not sound right to many people, but this is how I have been leading my life. My philosophy is that if I perform better, the leaders will acknowledge my work and promote or reward me if they find me deserving. I was responsible for my job and assumed that handling promotions and rewards are the leaders' jobs. I thought, "Why should I bother about them?" However, if I realize I am being taken for granted, I raise my voice.

I feel pleased with whatever awards I have received so far, and I do not assign any weightage to them. However, if someone respects my work, I should respect their acknowledgment too.

THE CRISIS PHASE

I have a different view of crises, challenges, and struggles. If I decide to walk on a particular path or if I aspire to accomplish something in my life, it is my responsibility to understand that it is a process, and there could be several challenges inherently or anthropogenically introduced during this process. In such cases, it is not a struggle; it is natural, and I should not complain about it or claim that I am struggling with something I decided to do. When we walk on a path, the world does not pause; it also moves at its own pace. Therefore, we should be aware that there could be some obstacles we may not have considered.

"For me, a struggle is the process of improving our capabilities to face any life challenges that may require having control over our emotions, enhancing patience, becoming intellectual and wise, and believing in responding to the situations we are put in rather than reacting to them."

However, the social perception of struggle is different and very subjective. Generally, people plan to accomplish many things in life and expect a smooth path, but whenever they find even a tiny hurdle, they start crying that they are struggling. Many socially perceived struggles exist, but I will skip writing about them. During my school and college days, I did not label it a struggle if I had to study for longer hours to perform better in classrooms or exams. Similarly, wherever I worked with any institutions, I never complained that I had a lot to work on, although I used to work exceptionally long hours sometimes. I considered them part of the job. There were instances when my dignity or principles were challenged. Then I had to handle them and in the case of a planned conspiracy against me, I had to make hard decisions. I have resigned thrice in my life so far, but they were not because I was forced to; instead, I completed my work and decided to resign, which I have not regretted so far. The best part is that the recipients of my resignations still respect me for my work and principles.

Therefore, I only share a few examples of extreme cases anyone experiences, i.e., economic crises and threats to survival in a foreign country where you are fighting alone. I want to highlight here that I do not want readers to perceive this book as a "victim's story," but instead as a warrior who knows that getting wounded is a part of any battle.

"I survived the worst phase where I was fighting alone on a foreign land, where the opponents were my country's people, not foreigners, and it was the foreigners who supported me a lot in this crisis."

11.1. The Economic Crisis

Since childhood, money has never been presented to us as the highest priority of our lives, so I never understood the definition of poor or rich. I only assumed that people with expensive clothing who own big houses and personal vehicles, and visit restaurants and hotels for expensive food are rich. I was okay with what I had; I never felt that whether I was rich or poor. I do not remember a single discussion in our family about our economic status in our society. I never felt less than anyone, and nothing but my morale was down because we were not financially sound then. Seeing ourselves as inferior to others triggers such thoughts, and we start comparing ourselves to many people.

The first economic crisis I can refer to is when I decided to go to the USA for my second Ph.D. I mentioned this in the previous section. However, I do not consider this a crisis because I decided to go to the USA, so I should have considered all aspects of this decision, especially knowing that I did not have savings nor were my parents financially capable of supporting me. Therefore, I am not considering this an economic crisis.

When I reached the USA, I knew I was by myself and had to be mentally prepared for any crisis. I never shared my challenges with my family as I did not want them to be worried about me. I had the habit of saving money, but at the same time, I had the habit of helping others who came to me for help. And I also had specific responsibilities and some liabilities too. Nevertheless, I never helped anyone by taking a loan from someone else, as I believe that if I am capable, then only I should be helping, even if that means I must curtail my needs, such as eating only once a day. My monthly income was approximately $1,100 and almost 45% of the amount was used for house rent and the rest for telephone, food, and commuting to the university. Still, I was saving a little amount so that I could take care of my responsibilities and liabilities. I did not feel bad when I lived in a room in a shared apartment, or a basement, or when all my colleagues bought a car, and neither did I feel bad when my colleagues ate whatever they wanted to eat. Those days, McDonald's had $1 McChicken, and I remember going to a McDonald's near my university and buying two or three McChickens; this was my food for 6-7 months. Indian food was costly in restaurants, so I used to go there only occasionally. Very soon my food crisis ended when I started to cook whatever I wanted to eat. I was devoted to my studies and research, and my economic state did not impact me. However, the most challenging days awaited me, and an economic crisis knocked on my door.

Only a few people know about the following incident. The period between my graduation with a Ph.D. in the USA and getting a job was one such crisis moment that I will never forget. I did not have money to pay my room rent or eat, and I could not share all these with my parents for two reasons. First, I never bothered anyone in my family with challenges in my life, and second, I knew they did not have money to support me. I desperately started looking for a job, and I saw one hope through a consulting firm. I applied there and got acceptance, including training and housing. It was a blessing that I felt I received directly from Lord Shiva. Before leaving my apartment, I had to meet my best friend's family, a Dominican family. My bank account was in the negatives, so I could not withdraw any money and had nothing in my pocket. I hesitated to ask my friend to pick me up or share that I had no money to catch a bus to go meet them.

While traveling back and forth from my university, many bus drivers knew me by face, so I thought maybe I could see if they could drop me at the bus stop closer to my friend's house. Luckily, one bus driver knew me, and I asked him whether he could drop me off.

He kindly said, "Sure, my friend!" I thanked him many times. After reaching my friend's house, we spent some time together, but Sister (my friend's wife) somehow read my face.

When I was about to leave, she said, "Brother, I do not have much money, but I would like to give you something as a blessing and wish." She then gave me $20. I was hesitant but also very emotional. Since we were a family, I took that $20 from her and returned home.

I also had to meet my American mother to seek her blessings. She is my Guru and mother. She is an African American who took care of me like her child. I always touch her feet whenever I meet her. I met her one day, and when I was about to leave, she very hesitantly asked if I would mind if she gave me something because she did not want to hurt my emotions unknowingly. I said, "Of course not, you are my Guru, and like a mother." Then she gave me $200. I was speechless. I wondered how she learned I needed money; I did not tell her anything about my financial condition.

That $220 still is very precious to me!

One day, I was in the university campus, and it was lunchtime; I had only a few bucks left in my wallet. So, I decided to buy a pizza slice from the canteen. I went there and ordered a slice of pizza.

When I was about to pay, the cashier said, "We are offering a free pizza only today for one person, and you are the chosen one. So, you do not have to pay; you are all set." Anyone can guess what I was feeling at that moment.

After some time, one student from the consulting training facility came to pick me up. That day, I had only $1 left in the hidden pocket of my wallet. I had no idea what was going to happen.

The only person I shared my situation with was my best friend in India, and he said, "Brother, even if I have to sell my house, I will, but you are not coming back empty-handed." That moment is unexplainable.

During this phase, I was not depressed or hopeless; I did nothing disgraceful to hold myself; I was only trying to catch Shiva's signals to understand what would happen and what I was supposed to do. Very soon, the day came when I got a data scientist job, and the phase ended. However, the challenges continued until I received my first paycheck. The salary I was offered then was good enough to survive and handle all my liabilities and responsibilities.

11.2. The Survival Challenge

For me, a survival challenge is when someone's dignity and life are at risk. There was a phase in my life where I could say that I experienced that I was fighting to survive. I was attacked from all sides; my career, dignity, integrity, and character were all at risk. Many people do not know about this phase of my life, only a couple, and they too know only bits and pieces. I was under extreme stress, and my primary thought was how my family would survive if something happened to me. I used to get scared with each e-mail, call, or message notification. Those fearful days continued for some time. One day, I thought about how long I could continue living in fear because the fear of losing everything in my life was terrifying and significantly impacted my health. I did experience several challenges in my life where I had to fight against several odds, and I never surrendered, but those were not comparable to my situation at this time. I was desperately looking for some guidance on how to face this challenge. At that time, I used to wear several gemstones on my fingers, and I started thinking maybe there was a misalignment between the planets and the stones. I was just trying to find answers outside. Then I started revisiting my past and trying to understand the patterns of my life. After deep introspection, I found one consistent answer: whenever I encountered any problem, my honesty helped me come out of it as a winner.

The other thought I had was that I was entirely devoted to lord Shiva, so I started debating if he knew my situation and if he had to make all the decisions, why was I getting scared thinking about stones and their impacts? I wanted to overcome all my fears. After a lot of internal debate, I realized that I would do my karma, and whatever happened, I would accept it as Shiva's blessings. So that day, I removed all the gemstones from my fingers. Then, I started focusing on the battle I was dragged into. My only objective was to defend myself, not attack. During this phase, two learnings were constantly around me: my father's teaching to "never give up" and my mother's teaching that "be yourself, and do not change according to people, only do your karma honestly;" I followed that.

The battle continued for over four months. Many supporters of my opponent were my so-called 'good friends.' I still remember supporting some of them when no one cared about them. Unfortunately, I was not experienced or equipped for this battle. However, I decided not to surrender; I fought that battle. More importantly, each day, I was calmer, more confident, and better prepared for the next day.

After four months of intense battle, I was calm but nervous when judgment day came.

While walking towards the battlefield, I received Lord Shiva's signal, "Son, do not worry; everything is going to be fine and positive." That gave me strength and confidence. When I reached the battleground, and the final round started, my opponent started attacking like a hopeless person; at that time, I experienced something outside of this world for the first time in my life.

I felt Goddess Saraswati telling me, "Son, just relax and let them attack; you do not even have to respond." I could not express what I felt then. So, I stayed quiet and did not launch any arsenal from my side. I was in complete peace with no stress, nothing; I was quietly observing what was happening. After some time, the battle was over, and the result was apparent I survived.

I would not say whether I won or lost; instead, I would say, "Dharma" defeated "Adharma" again! However, I was wounded as well, but that did not bother me as I considered that part of the battle.

However, I was told by my opponent that my career in the research field, especially in arsenic, would be destroyed. I am not sure how much that threat holds water, but the reality was that I did not get any academic or research positions in academia or with any big arsenic research group. Nevertheless, despite all these things, I did not give up my passion for research, and I have continued my research and authored 50 peer-reviewed articles, books, and book chapters, of which 19 are on arsenic, and many more are in the pipeline!

Since then, I did not put any gemstones, not because I do not believe the scientific reasons behind it but to improve my spiritual ability to directly connect to Lord Shiva and reduce dependencies on any other sources.

If I had to summarize my survival crisis journey, I would state that I survived because I did my work with honesty and dedication and fought my battle with honesty. My opponent knew they would never be able to challenge my work as I always do it honestly and with dedication. Therefore, they used a global model of defeating an enemy, i.e., defaming, and personal attack on character, attack on career, brutally attacking morale, and attempting all means to break the confidence and force to such an extent that instead of defending, I end up committing a mistake. Then, they will use these mistakes to prove that I am a serial offender.

What happened during this phase when I compared it with several other circumstances in my life or anybody else's life across the globe, I found many other people or groups applied similar approaches to destroy their opponents. So, my opponent used a global model to defeat me. I do not know whether there is a training center for learning such models or if it is the soul which, by nature, knows the models. I am still surprised at how I survived!

In this battle, I received support from people I did not even think would support me. It was clear to me that a divine power was helping me.

"In a battle between Dharma and Adharma, Dharma wins, but both get wounded."

THE SECRET

I did not plan my life; Lord Shiva designed it. Therefore, I did not know what strategy to follow if I encountered any severe challenge. But life teaches you lessons and provides opportunities to be a better version of ourselves by overcoming our weaknesses. Consequently, we get prepared to face challenges coming our way. Each individual responds or reacts to challenges differently, which means there is not necessarily a fixed model that could be applied to all challenges. However, those models help others be aware and adapt to their situations. I am unsure whether this is a secret as many people may have similar experiences and may have handled it the same way I did. Therefore, I share what helped me survive during the most challenging phases of my life, strictly during my journey as a scientist.

12.1. Soul Cleansing

When we aspire to do something purely based on our decision, we do not let the world know or seek their consent. That means the world runs according to its plans, and we do as we decide. Consequently, we may cross each other's paths, leading to conflict.

In such cases, the gravity of the conflict decides whether it will turn into a challenge or can be ignored. In the case of non-ignorable challenges, we have two options: surrender to the challenge or stand to face it. Now, this could be a turning point in our lives. If we surrender, we will keep surrendering for the rest of our lives, and if we decide to fight back, we must be mentally prepared for any unexpected hurdles in our path.

12.1.1. Realization

It depends on your honesty whether you are fighting for right or wrong. Therefore, if your conscience says that you are fighting for the right cause, then you must remember one thing: in this process, the first and the most important thing is you realize your own mistakes and then you must start preparing yourself for the battle. The journey of soul-cleansing starts with admitting to our own mistakes and releasing or overcoming the negative energy we possess. The realization could be related to the mistakes you may have committed during a particular challenge or throughout your life. Here, we need to understand that whatever we do has some response or reaction. Therefore, if we do something wrong, that will bring consequences to us sooner or later. Hence, you should try your best to recognize any mistakes you have made in the past. Although you may have committed mistakes unintentionally, they are still mistakes as the world looks at the act and not the intent. At this stage, you may want to revisit your life and try to identify all possible wrongs you may have done. However, it would be difficult to remember and create an inventory of all of them. So, it is wise to accept all the mistakes you have committed knowingly or unknowingly. But, most importantly, focus on your immediate challenge and figure out where you are a defaulter. The first step of realization will give you immense peace and strength to fight. The more realization you have, the more negative energy you release, creating a vacuum in your soul to attract positive energy; therefore, soul cleansing starts working.

12.1.2. Acceptance

Accepting the realized mistakes is the first success in soul-cleansing. Of course, it is not easy to accept your mistakes. But the moment you accept them, you will feel like you have started receiving positive energy and feeling lighter. Of course, there is a fine line between realization and acceptance, you may recognize that you have made mistakes or did wrong, but your pride, arrogance, or superiority will not let you accept that you can also commit mistakes or do wrong to someone else.

"Remember, there is a difference between what we think of ourselves and what we do. We may think of good things, but we do not necessarily do the same. This is a huge barrier in accepting our wrongs."

12.1.3. Surrender to the Divine Energy

Although people may identify as non-believers or atheists, at the end of the day, everybody realizes that there is a divine energy that runs the universe. Unfortunately, there were incidences when I also lost my trust in such divine energy. However, I immediately realized I was wrong. Even if you only believe in karma, you must know that for every action (force) in nature, there is an equal and opposite reaction. Therefore, whether the reaction will happen immediately or later is just a matter of time. If you believe in only divine energy or karma, you still follow the same principles. In any state of mind, force in nature is common. Hence, you should surrender to that divine energy force and continue doing your karma. The moment you surrender to the divine energy, it starts guiding you, and you start receiving signals on what to do next.

12.1.4. Overcoming All Fears

When you are being attacked, you have many questions and fears: what if you die, or what if your response may injure your opponent, what if you lose your dignity, what if you are portrayed as a flawed human being, and so on. All these scenarios are speculations created in our brains in our thought processes. Ideally, nothing happened; whatever happened is all our imagination. I remember my father always saying that if you are in trouble, expect the worst and be mentally prepared to face it, but never surrender yourself. Therefore, your realization and acceptance will give you enough strengths to overcome all your fears, and the moment you attain this state, you are already a winner in that battle.

12.1.5. Follow Brahmacharya Dharma

Brahmacharya is an integral part of ancient Indian culture. However, with time, the concept has strictly been tied to maintaining sexual celibacy. Nevertheless, it is not what and how it is currently perceived; one can get the details from various ancient Indian scriptures or real Gurus. For me, it is controlling your 'Kama' (lust for anything) and bringing purity and simplicity in thought processes, conversations, behaviors, and lifestyle. That exactly means that you control your negative energy and nurture your positive energy. To do all this, you do not have to go to any religious place; if you go, that's fine, but it is unnecessary. Without a Guru, I started doing everything by myself as if some divine energy was instructing me.

My journey may be criticized, but I did not do anything thinking that one day I would write an autobiography and hence design everything the world may want to see and appreciate. The entire phase was purely raw—an experience I had never in my life had before, so I continued going with the flow of the signals I was receiving.

In this phase, you are the most significant challenge for yourself. Yes, you meaning the nature and behavior you possess because you must fight with your nature and behaviors, which have been with you for several years, that you have practiced each second. Trust me; this is the most painful process. I am not trying to discourage anyone; it is what it is. To win a survival battle, you must work hard, put in all your sincere efforts, and utilize all the knowledge and experiences you have acquired over several years. Following Brahmacharya has several other advantages too.

12.1.6. Be courageous

When you overcome your fears and start practicing Brahmacharya Dharma, you will feel the strength to face anything. You will start responding to each attack fearlessly, one by one. In this state, you are ready to fight the world because of the power of truth, honesty, and positive energy. My body weight was almost half what it used to be a couple of months ago, but my confidence and courage were multiple times than they used to be. I would say I experienced a new 'Sushant' in me.

12.1.7. Learn Forgiveness

There is a famous line by a renowned Indian poet, Late Ramdhari Singh Dinkar "क्षमा शोभती उस भुजंग को जिसके पास गरल हो उसको क्या जो दंतहीन विषरहित, विनीत, सरल हो।" from his famous poem "कुरुक्षेत्र." Coincidently, he was also from Bihar, and his native village was not too far from mine. The line has a broad meaning in the context of Mahabharata and Ramayana, where the poet explains that only the powerful have the privilege to forgive someone. I do not intend to compare myself with any of the characters portrayed by the poet. I only want to convey that I was the most vulnerable person then, but the entire journey of soul cleansing helped me emerge as the most potent responder of my opponents. In this journey, my only goal was to defend myself, not to attack my opponents. I did my homework and collected all the pieces of evidence that could defend me. However, in this process, I was also able to collect all shreds of evidence that could destroy them as well. Although the evidence against my opponents was only a click away, I decided to forgive them, not take revenge, or attack. So, my focus was only on defending myself.

"Revenge will destroy you first before it destroys your opponents, so never think of taking revenge. Everybody receives the 'equal and opposite reaction of their karma,' so let time decide their destiny. Do not try to become another God."

12.1.8. Continue the Soul-cleansing Journey

The soul-cleansing journey is endless and must continue; hence, do not think you can stop this process, and you will be safe for the rest of your life. This entire process will prepare you to face any challenges in your life. Additionally, it will bring clarity, confidence, compassion, and peace to your life.

On the contrary, it is easy to follow the other path, i.e., surrendering to the challenge. You will rise and may achieve whatever you aspire for, but you will keep losing yourself every day, and at the end of the day, you become a characterless human being because you lost your human character. The choice is always yours.

"If you follow dharma, you will likely have to struggle a lot, but ultimately dharma wins."

Remember, what I explained above is not a crash course for you. I did not take any training during that period. Instead, I have presented it in its raw form the best I could by recalling those incidences and experiences after several years.

I kept highlighting that we all need a Guru to guide us to become good human beings and succeed in our professional and personal lives. Therefore, please try your best to find such a Guru.

12.2. Be Your Own Guru

Since 2015, I have worked full-time in the industry where finding time even for myself was extremely difficult. The biggest question everybody around me has is about how I managed my time to continue my research activities. It is not something I consider incredible. Instead, it was a natural day-to-day activity outside my office hours.

Although I always enjoyed what I did, that does not mean I always got the work I liked. Instead, I started developing an interest in those works. On the other hand, teaching and research have been my passion, so I never lost interest in scientific investigations. I also took several lectures during the night or early morning and simultaneously worked on several research projects. Furthermore, since I have been living alone, I could utilize all my out-of-office hours and vacations for teaching and research.

The next question was how I switched between my job and passion. The answer is that I utilized my teaching and research skills in my job and vice-versa. This is why I learned how academic research could be translated into industrial products. The other questions come from how I managed everything daily. I must admit that I sleep less and push myself too much to accommodate research activities.

"I believe that our body functions according to the way we train our brain. So, I started utilizing my brain more than I usually used to. Therefore, my job and research activities became natural to me and they never had any conflict, rather they complimented each other."

I have been a dedicated professional at work and a dedicated scientist outside my job hours. With time, I kept pushing myself to do more and more. Therefore, I have never stopped being creative or innovative at work and when I do science. Therefore, I cannot say I do not have time for research. Instead, I think about how to expand my brain's capabilities to do more in lesser time.

Only my teachers or classmates can comment on what kind of student I was, but one thing I can claim is how to apply my knowledge and skills to various topics and domains. I still remember the concepts or the topics I used to think about 5-10 years ago; people have just begun working on them. I am not claiming that I am a genius or that others are short-visioned; I am only telling the truth. But I still believe that if I had a Guru, I would have been a better version of myself because I know what I lack and where to improve. The only thing in my control is learning more, working hard, and being consistent, which I always try to do.

Since childhood, I have consistently searched for a Guru who could show me the correct path, answer all my questions, help me reduce ambiguities in my thought processes and understanding of life, and inspire me to keep improving myself as an individual. My mother has been playing the role of a Guru. However, my dimensions have been broad, such as life, science, spirituality, and connecting to Lord Shiva. As a result, I have always dedicated myself to all who entered my life, whether as teachers, colleagues, or friends. I learned a lot from them, but my journey to find a Guru did not end. In this journey, I started understanding myself very well: who I am, what I am, why I am, what I want to do, why I want to do, and who could guide me in the journey of becoming a better version of myself. I realized that since childhood I was naturally attracted to Shiv Ji, and when I started learning about his life, I started imbibing his character, which made me realize that he is my Guru. Since then, I have started getting all my questions answered by him during my regular conversations with him whenever I meditate. I am pretty sure that readers may not be able to digest these things; therefore, the guru mantra I have for them is:

"Be your own Guru and try to connect with the divine energy if you believe in it. Even if you do not believe in it, try cleansing your soul. That will help you catch the signals nature wants to send you. All these will help you become a better version of yourself and succeed in life."

You can give instructions to yourself and ask to do specific work. Take the example of your workplace and when you are asked to do something you do not like or to work extra, either off hours or during weekends or holidays. You usually follow those instructions, pushing yourself a little extra to complete that work. You can become your own boss and instruct yourself to push yourself extra to follow your passion, and you will experience a change in your life. Honestly assess yourself and try listing your limitations, then try teaching yourself as your Guru and set small goals to achieve them. And, never stress too much if you cannot finish them; remember, it is a process that will take time. The goal is not to add extra stress to your life but to expand your capabilities and abilities to do multiple things by taking command of your brain in your hands.

"The two Guru-mantras which I followed consistently helped me to come out of trouble successfully. The first Guru-mantra, "Never give up," was instilled by our father to us, and the second Guru-mantra, "Be yourself," was instilled by our mother. My mother always kept telling and teaching me that whatever happens, I should be myself, need not change myself according to people, keep walking the path of truth, be honest, and never hurt anyone even if they hurt me."

THE SPIRITUAL PROGRESSION

Since childhood, I have had a natural attraction toward Lord Shiva. When I realized spirituality, I started following Shiva as my Guru and God! There are several instances I felt his presence. I started imitating his life, becoming patient day by day, engulfing all the odds coming my way, and responding to all challenges with a broad smile. Unfortunately, I did not have and still do not have any spiritual Guru who could show me the path of spirituality. So, I started directly connecting with Lord Shiva to seek inspiration. However, I used to practice meditation during my college days. There are some secrets I cannot disclose, but I can only share that during my undergraduate days, I attained a very high-level meditation state. Unfortunately, because of the lack of awareness, I could not continue it. I still think if I had a spiritual guru, I would have reached the highest level of meditation by now.

The survival crisis phase (section 11) played a significant role in advancing me to spirituality. For me, spirituality is to continue doing your karma, stay connected with Lord Shiva daily, get all open questions answered when connecting with him, and try overcoming all negative energies of our personality. This journey has been a roller-coaster. Finally, I reached a level where I could connect with nature and the cosmos energy. All changes happened internally and are still in progress. Recently, I also started reading the Vedas and Bhagwat Geeta. This path is not easy and feels like climbing a high straight mountain where at each step, there is a high likelihood that you may fall. I would say my spiritual journey has just begun.

"Everybody's spiritual journey is unique. So, instead of wasting time on criticizing others, start criticizing yourself and do the best you can to become a better version of yourself."

14

CHALLENGES TO BECOMING SCIENTISTS

$\mathcal{B}$ecoming a scientist is not an easy path. However, individuals' level of commitment, patience level, and motivation to do good science could guide their path to becoming a scientist. It may not sound natural in the current era if someone thinks becoming a scientist is a good profession, and they can earn money, name, and fame, and then they get the motivation to become a scientist, they should better stop walking on that path right now.

"Being a scientist is a responsibility, not a profession, and unless you believe in it, you will end up dropping in the middle of your research or becoming a publication machine. Consequently, science will leave us far behind. Furthermore, once one overcomes their inherent human limitations, society has many more well-established challenges waiting for them. Therefore, they should know this before deciding to become a scientist."

It is not to scare or make anyone afraid of choosing this path but to make them aware of making informed decisions and not regretting later.

The challenges listed below are more or less everywhere to various degrees. However, it should not be perceived as an attempt to generalize but to make the next generations aware of the deep-rooted challenges.

14.1. Research Culture

I would not hesitate to write that there has been a significant lack of research culture in Bihar and around. It was around 2004 when I was conducting research in the laboratories and the field. I used to read research articles even if I had access to only the abstracts of most good publications. I was also looking for scientists around me, and I hardly used to find one or two who could inspire me to do science.

"Teachers and scientists are different in training and temperament. Not all faculty members need to be good scientists and vice-versa. Therefore, those faculty who are good scientists should only be guiding scholars."

Undoubtedly, there were great faculty members but not necessarily great scientists. While pursuing my Master's and Ph.D. in India, I met many professors and scientists and attended several national and international conferences. Either my expectation as a scientist was extraordinarily high, or I did not know who precisely is a scientist!

Till now, I have been active in academic and research activities and I did meet several students from India and abroad. My observation about the lack of research culture was the same, with a couple of exceptions. I have encountered several people working in the labs, but the soul of a scientist was missing somewhere. People around influence us, forming a culture around them that newcomers imitate. Therefore, new scholars will learn and follow if a research group has established a good research culture. A good research culture can transform a mediocre student into a good scientist and vice-versa.

Even after two decades, I found no significant change in the research culture in Bihar; it declined. I also see a lack of sound policies to solve these challenges. Many professors local to the institutions in Bihar became active in politics or secured higher positions within or outside the academic systems. However, those faculty members who wanted to do research were ignored, discouraged, and demotivated greatly. The irony is that institutions get recognition and awards because of the contributions of those hardworking faculty members who invest their time and resource to conduct good research.

I still remember one administrative officer appointed by the then Governor of Bihar who started reforming the state's teaching and research culture. However, he got transferred in a few months, and the reform died there. Since then, the situation has been more or less the same. In 2021-2022, I met several students and scholars, and I did not see a better research culture, sense of science, and awareness of responsibility as a scientist. Of course, I do not hold students responsible for such situations. They need proper guidance that the faculty members could not do well.

"There is a need for strong policy enforcement to eliminate those faculty members from academia who do not produce and promote good research. Furthermore, accreditation agencies should review faculty members' academic and research profiles before rating the institutions."

14.2. Research Ethics

Ethics are taught and instilled during childhood; teaching ethics to an adult would be challenging. However, research ethics have certain elements that require training and they should be appropriately conveyed to each researcher. It should be part of the curriculum. Many researchers I met in formal or informal settings or through media found research ethics alien to them. I do not think it was their fault. The research environments play a crucial role in instilling good research values and ethics. Many may have earned their Ph.D. degrees without even conducting any research and many would have published someone else's work and many more examples that do not suit the research world. If someone starts investigating all these, it may likely turn into a bloody investigation because many such people may hold high positions in and outside the state. They will try everything to protect their positions and pride. Therefore, it is not a good idea to dig graves but instead focus on how this can be fixed to secure future generations.

The rest of the world is not untouched by this disease; hijacking others' work, publications based on fabricated data, plagiarizing others' work, and many more such unethical reports have been published in several mainstream magazines and journals. It will be extremely challenging to prevent this problem as it has widely spread worldwide.

14.3. Efficient Research Advisors

As I mentioned in the previous sections, not all good faculty members are efficient research advisors; I believe this is a global phenomenon. There is a contemporary culture of hiring graduating Ph.D. scholars as assistant professors who can guide Ph.D. students. As a result, thousands of scholars either could not complete their Ph.D., their research got hijacked, or they were exploited in several ways. I have encountered several scholars worldwide who were on the cosmos because their advisors had no idea what they should be doing or how. Many scholars had to change their advisors and the topics they had already spent a few years on. The inefficiency could be in several categories. However, this is not the intent of this book. We genuinely need efficient research advisors, valid for Bihar and worldwide. In a nutshell, if newly hired faculties do not know science and research, how will they produce good researchers or scientists?

"The culture of mentorship for scientific advancement is not given significance in scientific institutions worldwide and I desire to see these changes right before my eyes during my lifetime."

14.4. Laboratory Resources

When I started my research, I knew that laboratory facilities are costly; therefore, I was not expecting anything out of the blue. I could complete all my experiments using whatever instruments I had available. However, the operations and maintenance of instruments depend on the research culture of our laboratory. I learned that other institutions had many analytical instruments that never came out of the boxes because of the lack of maintenance. Still, I would say that there is a lack of high-quality laboratories.

Additionally, there is a lack of trained lab technicians who can operate and maintain laboratory instruments. Although researchers are supposed to be trained to handle the instruments, they should also know at least the basics of the operation and maintenance of those instruments. However, such breeds are significantly fewer but needed to advance science. I have been involved in purchasing analytical instruments, operation, and maintenance in the laboratory I worked in India. In the USA, I did learn about several new analytical instruments and how to troubleshoot them if there were any technical issues. However, there was technical support from the instrument providers if the instruments required heavy maintenance.

Moreover, it depends on whether scholars who work in the laboratories are interested in learning proper operations and troubleshooting laboratory equipment. Again, all these come with research culture in the lab or the scientific temperament of researchers. We did not have an air-conditioned lab in India, but we used all laboratory facilities for quality research work then. In the USA, the laboratories were in the best possible condition. I hardly saw professors in India visiting and working in the Indian labs. This is why I distinguish between faculty members and scientists. In India, you could find good faculty members who may be excellent in knowledge and teaching skills, but in the USA, most professors were equally excellent in teaching and research. I have seen the head of departments and the college dean working in their laboratories in the USA. On the contrary, in India, you will not see the head of the departments, principals, or the college dean working in laboratories or involved in any research activities, not even teaching.

"Students imbibe their teachers' characters; therefore, in any institution where teachers lack scientific temperament, it is almost impossible for the institutions to produce good scientists."

14.5. Library Facilities

The library is the key to storing and disseminating current and past scientific investigations and outcomes. Having an extensive library building is not enough as it requires the availability and accessibility of good books and journals relevant to the research activities being conducted at the colleges, institutions, or universities. When I started my research in Bihar, there was a severe lack of availability and accessibility to scientific journals. I used to write to scientists asking them to send their full publications as I could not access most of the articles relevant to my research. One can read my Ph.D. thesis, where I have acknowledged all those scientists who shared their publications whenever I requested them. I could say that I had support from all those scientists who were not around me and who let me feel that if there is a will, there is a way! Now the situation is different, and we live in an Open Access world where most scientific literature is freely available to all researchers worldwide. In the USA university, books and scientific journals were available and accessible. All these played a significant role in my research studies in the USA. I think, in current times, libraries should not be a constraint for any researchers, whether in Bihar or anywhere else in the world.

14.6. Lack of Resources

I never believed that resources could stop anyone from thinking about science, becoming a scientist, and putting sincere efforts toward achieving it. However, underprivileged students still need support to become scientists as this path is longer than any other profession.

As I mentioned in the previous section, we come from a very humble family, so it was very challenging for me to choose a career with a long path and no guarantee of a high-paid salary. I was lucky to receive doctoral assistantships for both of my Ph.D. degrees. However, I still needed a significant amount to go to the USA. My parents had some savings, but they were not enough, and I also did not want to put any financial burden on them at this stage of their life. Therefore, I tried getting an education loan from a national bank. Initially, I was told I would get the loan as I had a full scholarship; however, it disappointed me and wasted my time. By now, I had no time to look for any other banks. So, I started reaching out to the friends I trusted the most. As I said, there is a way if there is a will. As I did not want to bother any of my friends or make them uncomfortable, I was cautious about whom to contact. I did not have many options. So first, I reached out to one of my friends who was rich and could afford to lend me the amount I needed. I immediately realized my friend got uncomfortable, so I did not bother again. Then, I reached out to two of my friends. My first friend deposited three months of his salary into my account; he had been waiting for his salary for three months that he had just got. The other friend also helped me. I cannot forget that my friend's wife, who is like a sister to me, went to the bank in the scorching heat to deposit the amount. These two friends supported me when I needed to reach the USA for my 2nd Ph.D. I want to clarify that I have a special place for these friends in my heart, but I do not have any negative feelings for anyone I reached out to seek support, including the banks and the people.

"My suggestion to all Ph.D. aspirants is that when you decide to walk on a certain path, you should be aware of the challenges during that journey. So, it is not wise to blame anyone who may not have helped, supported, or played a negative character during your journey. The best policy is never to give up or blame others if something unexpected happens."

14.7. Language Barrier

It was the time when I applied for a research position at one of the top research institutions in India. There was a telephone interview scheduled. I did not have a cell phone then and I had to call from a telephone booth. I was very nervous for various reasons, including the high reputation of the institution, attending an interview right after work, the environment of the telephone booth, and the English language. The interview started with my introduction, and I started fumbling.

Before I could continue, the interviewer stopped me right there and said, "You cannot even introduce yourself properly, then how you will work?" I was stunned at that moment. The interview did not last for more than a couple of minutes. I took the blame on myself that maybe I needed to practice the English language more. However, so many other essential questions kept haunting me about why I was not even asked a single question on the topic, why the interviewer did not give me a few seconds to calm down, or what made the interviewer rude to me after reviewing my good profile. I also started thinking, was the English language the reason for all this? I know that at that time, I was not very fluent in English communication, I still cannot claim that I have mastered English, but the mode of communication in all my education, research, teaching, and job was in English only. I did not have one clear answer, and I was looking for the real cause behind it so I could work on it to improve myself. This one incident had a significant impact on me. I started debating whether I would have responded the same way if the interview had been in my mother tongue or the national language, Hindi. This debate was useless as I was not even asked a single question on the topic. Still, I thought at least I would have been very confident that day. That day I did not know that I would be put in a world where English would be the primary language for writing and speaking.

Later, I worked with a non-profit supported by a Korean group, where I used to translate the organization's head's speeches from English to Hindi during community meetings. Then, I worked with UNICEF, where all communication was only in English. Of course, all these experiences were in non-research environments. Nevertheless, the days were not too far when my research communication skills were tested before research legends.

It was in 2006 when I went to participate in the world's biggest conference on Arsenic issues in New Delhi, India. The principal investigator of our Project Arsenic was kind enough to offer me to present our research paper (Figure 22).

Figure 22. Presenting arsenic research at my first International Conference before the world's top arsenic scientists.

World's top arsenic scientists were sitting in front of me, and I presented our research work on Arsenic in Bihar, India, and of course, the presentation was in English. The presentation was appreciated. I believe they evaluated my research, not my English communication skills.

Figure 23. Presentation in China at an Asian Cross-Cultural Conference in 2009.

After a few years, I went to China for a global cross-cultural conference as one of the Indian representatives. Again, I presented my work in English (Figure 23). However, there was a presentation by one research group, and the author presented their work in Chinese but almost none in the hall could understand as most of us were non-Chinese. He was asked to present in English, but he denied saying that he could not do that as if he did, he would lose the importance of the work. This incident was highly annoying and disrespectful at that moment for the audience. However, I appreciated the presenter because that work was essential for them, and the community they worked with spoke the local Chinese language, not English.

After a couple of years, I had the opportunity to present one of my first Ph.D. research at Yale University, USA, at a global conference (Figure 24).

Figure 24. Poster presentation of my first Ph.D. research at Yale University, USA, at a global conference in 2010.

After the conference, when I came outside the venue, one scientist started interacting with me. She was a senior professor.

She asked me, "Where are you from?" I said that I was from India and she appreciated my work and communication with her in English. Of course, I did not expect such a comment, but it felt good. Maybe I was getting better at communicating in English.

"The journey as a scientist was not to master communication in a foreign language, but in the research areas."

The above examples are critical to understanding one of the core problems for aspiring scientists in India. I did not even get the opportunity to continue my interview probably because I could not speak well in English, another person did not feel ashamed presenting their work in their native language, and a native English speaker appreciates a non-native English speaker.

I met many brilliant students who lacked English communication skills. If they could speak and write in their native languages, we would have many more outstanding contributions to the scientific world.

India's recent Nation Educational Policy is highly appreciable as it promotes education in regional languages. However, I want to advise students never to feel less or inferior because their English communication is not as good as others; instead, the focus must be on their subject.

"Learning new languages is always good, but language is merely a tool to communicate your ideas. Do not let science die inside you because of the language barrier."

One global language is required internationally but should not become necessary for scientists' success. In India and maybe other developing countries, most brilliant and hardworking students come from a socioeconomic group who may not be able to afford to study in English medium schools. Therefore, they primarily depend on government schools and colleges. If teachers are qualified, they can train students in the English language. However, in Bihar, corruption is so deeply rooted in teachers' recruitment in government schools and colleges that it is a herculean task to prepare students for doing science at government schools or colleges. Moreover, teachers in government schools and colleges cannot even write and speak good Hindi; English is a considerable burden. Therefore, instead of forcing them to learn a foreign language, they should be encouraged to improve their mother tongue.

14.8. The Reservation System

Faculty members are hired based on their castes and religion, requiring below-average academic scores. Fifteen percent of seats are reserved for Scheduled Castes, 7.5% seats are reserved for Scheduled Tribes for Assistant Professor, Associate Professor, and Professor positions, and 27% for Other Backward Classes for Assistant Professor position only[3]. They also have age relaxations and require 5% fewer marks in their academic degrees [4]. On top of that, they enjoy the benefits of the reservation system even after the recruitment, such as promotions. Recently, the Indian government has reserved 10% of seats for economically weaker

---

[3]https://www.ugc.gov.in/pdfnews/6320608_reservation-Policy.pdf
[4]http://www.maitreyi.ac.in/DataFiles/Tender/09886620232225105151227Asstt.%20Prof.%20(Advertisement).pdf

sections (EWS) of upper-caste students. Therefore, approximately 40% of seats are available for upper-caste students on merit. One can imagine that a faculty member with lower performance in their academics earned a Ph.D. degree, became a professor, and guided the next generations in research. Many people may argue that grades do not decide anyone's intellect, which is true, but what about students with higher scores who need to fight for 1 or 2 seats instead of students in reservation categories who have their seats reserved?

The reservation system in India became more a political than social issue and it was supposed to be stopped decades ago. However, no politicians dare to fix this as this will lead to substantial social unrest because most politicians and people do not want to give up this fortune; it is their bread and butter. If the reservation system will not be amended and should be based only on economic status, this will never let India grow.

This conversation may become a serious debate as no one wants to discuss or fix this problem, so it is better to leave it to the next generations as I do not see any politicians or social activists having the courage to take up this issue to a logical closure. Therefore, India awaits a courageous and honest leader to take charge and mitigate this chronic challenge.

"The reservation system in India has forced 'bright brains' to migrate outside their states and country, significantly impacting the country's development."

It is a general understanding among Indian netizens and others worldwide that the reservation system only benefits Hindu communities. However, it is beyond that; minorities also benefit from it. More importantly, the Hindu community of India has consistently been under sponsored mass religious conversions by both Christian and Muslim groups and organizations. Because of the corruption and loopholes in the reservation policies, people who convert from Hinduism to Islam or Christianity also expect to continue availing the benefits of reservation as they used to avail before the conversion in the reservation caste categories. There is a unique case where the Madras high court of India rejected the backward quota claim of a man who converted to Islam from Hinduism[5]. The man was originally a Hindu and belonged to a reservation category. Later, he converted to Islam and wanted the caste reservation benefit for a government job. Caste or religion-based reservation system in recruitment and promotion is a chronic issue that requires careful mitigation policies.

"The reservation system based on caste and religion is a severe challenge in India in general and, in particular, for nurturing and retaining good scientists within India."

The reservation system is not only in India but also in developed countries, such as the USA. Unfortunately, it is spreading, and other categories are getting added, such as gender and sexual orientation. I do not see it ending soon; it is an organized industry. Large global organizations, such as the United Nations and others, are known for ensuring equality among various socio-economic groups, but I do not see it happening. Instead, society has been split into various categories. Such categorizations benefit a large population; therefore, no one wants to give up that fortune. Unfortunately, such a reservation system has invaded academia

---

[5]'One Can't Carry His Caste After Conversion': Madras High Court Rejects Backward Quota Claim Of Man Who Converted To Islam From Hinduism (livelaw.in)

and other industries, which is extremely dangerous for humans in the coming days. Several intellectually awakened individuals worldwide have realized this problem and are putting their sincere efforts into making others understand the gravity of this issue. However, this is a herculean task for them as their opponents are mighty by all means.

14.9. The VIP Culture

Ancient India was Guru-driven, where science, society, economy, institutions, and politics were inspired and supported by scientists, including but not limited to Aryabhata (mathematician-astronomer), Maharishi Charak (Father of Ancient Indian Science of Medicine), Maharishi Sushruta (founding father of surgery), Maharishi Patanjali (Father of Yoga), and Nagarjuna (metallurgist and alchemist). Later, Vishnugupt, popularly known as Acharya Chanakya (author of the Artha-shastra- the Science of Material Gain), and many other scholars nurtured the scientific temperament of Indians. However, their glory started fading with time and the reason was the people. However, frequent invasions and destruction of India began. Moreover, all these could not suppress the scientific temperament of Indians. As a result, India continued to produce several geniuses, such as Chandrasekhara Venkata Raman (a Nobel Laurette of Physics), Homi Jehangir Bhabha (Quantum Physics), and Srinivasa Ramanujan (Mathematics). Even after the British colonization ended in India, the Indian soil did not stop producing brilliant scientists, such as Har Gobind Khorana (Nobel Prize for Physiology or Medicine with Marshall W. Nirenberg and Robert W. Holley) and Avul Pakir Jainulabdeen Abdul Kalam (Aerospace). The list is endless. Unfortunately, I have seen how scientists became mere frame materials, and in society, they could not become role models for young scientists. Jobs, power, and money started dominating the social psychic, and people passionate about science started taking up glamourless jobs only for 'nerds.'

If I remember, it was around 2008-2009 when I was addressing my undergraduate students on their farewell day; I promised them that I would prove that teaching and research is the most glamorous profession which means I knew the decline of teaching and research profession 14 years ago (Figure 25).

Figure 25. Addressing undergraduate students at their farewell party in 2009.

Unfortunately, I am still struggling as I am not working in academia where I could inspire the next generations to do great science. However, many of my former students work in academia in Indian and foreign institutions, meaning the science and scientists did not die.

One heartbreaking incident happened in 2019, when a genius mathematician, Dr. Vashishtha Narayan Singh (Padma Shri), died in Patna Medical College and Hospital of Bihar, India, where his family could not even get any support to bring his dead body gracefully back to their hometown. The scientist and science culture died again because of a dead silence among scientists, the state's political leaders, and the country.

"A culture does not die overnight; it takes time, support from the communities, systematic and consistent efforts from the destroyers, and a dead silence from the spineless individuals of that culture."

Each challenge listed in this book requires an independent book to capture how we reached this situation.

In the USA, the college dean and professors used to come to various seminars and presentations of college students and I never saw them having any bodyguards or having reserved seats in the seminar halls. Most of the time, they are found listening to students standing at the back of the seminar halls and no one used to get up to offer them a seat. It was not that students did not respect them; it was the culture; no one was a "very important person." Only science was substantial. On the contrary, you could find even college principals in Bihar, India walking with at least half a dozen people, including a gunman. Additionally, meeting the dean or vice-chancellors of the colleges and universities respectively is almost impossible. Principals and vice-chancellors are perceived as administrative posts in Indian colleges; therefore, nobody expects them to become a role-model of good teaching or research. They are the VIPs and the employees who are their favorites are not the scientists. Scientists are not VIPs, but politicians, doctors, high administrative officers, and celebrities are, and they significantly influence the next generations, discouraging them from choosing science as a career.

"When the positions and power dominate, knowledge gets suppressed. Therefore, the chairs and the people who hold that chair become VIPs."

I am very optimistic, but I do not see any significant change in this VIP culture in Bihar and India as a whole in at least a couple of decades.

14.10. Student Union and Administrative Support

I remember my college days in India, where the student unions were primarily motivated by political gains, not students' welfare. I confronted them several times whenever they came to end classes for some issue. I could not understand how abandoning classes would help students. Most student union leaders used to be either from non-science subjects, former students, or have been in colleges for ages. Confronting these people could lead to fights as they would physically attack students or anyone coming their way. When I started teaching, I remember a day when many boys (who claimed to be student union members) came to shut down a lab class I was taking. They thought I was also among the students, so they talked rudely with me. Only girls were in the lab that day, so I had to ensure nothing unpleasant happened to them. I asked all the students to enter the lab, and I started talking to those guys. I told those guys I was taking a lab class and that we could not abandon the experiments. They became very aggressive and wanted me to shut down the lab and close the classroom; then, I had no other option other than to become aggressive. I told them that I would not abandon the class and that if they had a problem meet me after the class gets over at 4 PM. I do not know what happened to them but they did not reappear. This is only one example and there are many more such incidents.

A recent case happened at India's one of the best universities, which is known for its good quality education and research, where a group of students led an anti-national movement on the university campus. All such incidents have a massive impact on students who want to study and become scientists. In any such cases, there is no administrative support for students.

During my Ph.D. in the USA, I was probably the first Indian who won an election (57% votes) and became the Chairperson of the Graduate Students Organization, where I served for two consecutive years. However, I never experienced such incidents there. Students used to bring their issues and ideas to us during our meetings and we used to bring them back to the administration.

There is a long list of academic issues that have never been addressed or resolved by any student association or administrative bodies.

"India needs 'students' unions,' not 'politically motivated students' gang.' Furthermore, India needs administrative officers who have respect for teachers and scientists, and are not motivated by personal gains and political power."

14.11. The White-Collar Criminals

Unfortunately, I must write this section. After all, it is essential to let the world know the ugly truth of the research world because not everybody dares to speak about these issues. In the state of Bihar, administrative delays by colleges and universities, irresponsible behaviors by faculty members and Ph.D. committees, and asking scholars for personal work could be experienced by several scholars. Asking female or male scholars to get involved in unethical acts is unthinkable; at least, I did not get to know about a single case in Bihar. Instead, girl scholars receive extra support and comfort. However, I did get to know from many scholars directly or indirectly that many of them share stories about several scholars whose advisors have exploited them in several ways. In India and other developing countries, speaking up for such acts by female students is perceived as women's fault, and in the end, they are the ones who suffer as they lose their dignity, but the culprit never gets punished. Women's dignity is priceless; therefore, this could be one of the reasons why those female scholars never speak up.

On the other hand, in the USA, scholars are very safe; at least they receive support from the university administrations. So, we can argue that if they do not speak, how would the world know what happened? My counterargument would be to create a monster-free system with no scope for such sins. However, there is another scenario where some scholars may also use all means possible to earn Ph.D. degrees, get good references, and secure jobs. It is hard to create a clean boundary to pinpoint where the faults lie. However, this is a critical issue to be discussed in scientific and social communities, so people can be aware of it. I may be biased towards students, so I do not hesitate to say that those faculty members are the culprits who exploit their students, and therefore, I name them "white-collar criminals." The victims are not only girls; many boys have committed suicide because of the misery they went through during their Ph.D. periods. Identifying and punishing those "white-collar criminals" should be of high priority, so no one dares to think about such sinful acts.

"Degree without dignity is worthless. Therefore, speak up and stand up for your dignity. If you do not, remember that you have added to such culture, and the next generations will have to go through this anguish again."

I am not writing it in detail as it will open a new can of worms. Instead, I would encourage investigative journalists to do such work and reveal the ugly faces of those monsters in academia. It is unfortunate to see news media not discussing these severe issues in India.

FUTURE ENDEAVORS

*T*o say that being a scientist in my future is more than just a pipe dream is an understatement. For me, it is more about spreading value and making a significant contribution to the field of research. The advancement of science is contingent on maintaining a steady stream of researchers who can generate and share knowledge for the advancement of science and improve the lives of the people in the area. This pipeline includes scientists at early and mid-career stages and senior scientists. Therefore, training and guidance are essential to the professional development of scientists in the early stages of their careers. Mentors are individuals who provide targeted assistance to promising young scientists to help them develop into research leaders. A competent mentor will assist the mentee in expanding their skill set, boosting their self-assurance, and developing new ideas that can be developed into research and development goals.

15.1. The CAIES Foundation

It is too late for me to return to any academic institution, hold a position, and then start nurturing the next generations of scientists. Therefore, I started a research foundation where I support them free of cost. I know it is not easy, but I never believed in anything easy. I always had to earn whatever I aspired to; therefore, I am taking each step accordingly. The Center for Artificial Intelligence and Environmental (CAIES) Foundation is dedicated to nurturing next-generation scientists in artificial intelligence and environmental sustainability. Readers can get more details from the website (https://caienvsus.org/). I have also started the world's first scholarship for arsenic research through the foundation. Furthermore, I am starting a subsequent scholarship to nurture young brains in science, dedicated to the late Dr. Vashishtha Narayan Singh.

A FEW WORDS FOR THE NEXT GENERATION OF SCIENTISTS

I am neither a Nobel laureate nor a celebrity that people would listen to, but I trust that at least one person will benefit from my journey and may become a legendary scientist. Of course, everybody's path is unique and may not apply to others. However, the core philosophy of one individual may help others too. So, my last few words to next-generation scientists are:

- Socioeconomic background should not become a bottleneck for anyone. I already broke that and so can others.

- Resource challenges should never discourage anyone else from moving forward, just as I never stopped. Therefore, continue your science journey; many good souls are out there who could support you.

- The lack of support from research advisors should not encourage anyone to put all the blame on the advisor's shoulder and get away with nothing. So, if I succeeded, anybody else can achieve that too.

- I did not get the opportunity to continue my scientific journey in academic or scientific institutions, but I did not let die a scientist within me. So, others can also keep their spirit alive.
- With all challenges, if I can earn two Ph.D. degrees within ten years, anybody else can earn theirs too; they have no reason to drop out unless it is a life and death situation.
- If I can continue researching and publishing, even being in the industry, anybody else can do it too.
- We may not get opportunities for what we aspired for, so there are several ways of utilizing the knowledge and skills we have learned. Hence, learn how to complement what you got and what your passion is.

"The bottom line is that becoming a scientist is not easy, but once you start walking this path, never disappoint yourself by quitting in the middle; it is a sin."

Also, speak up whenever you find yourself in a situation where you are getting exploited by anyone. If you do not speak up, you are nurturing that culture and adding to the misery that the next generations must experience. Girls must speak up, and there is no point in earning a degree at the cost of your dignity.

I will also encourage students who have compromised at several levels to get their research papers published or earn Ph.D. degrees to be courageous and come forward to support other vulnerable students.

"You should have a good journey to share with the next generations, even if it is full of challenges, but not a compromised journey. So, please SPEAK UP, NEVER BACKDOWN, and NEVER SURRENDER!"

India will become a "Vishwa Guru" if science and scientists are adequately nurtured. So, there is a need to foster 'Gurus' by bringing the 'Gurukul' system back to Indian society.

REFERENCES

Chakraborti, D, Sushant K Singh, Md Harunur Rashid, and Mohammad Mahmudur Rahman. 2011. "Arsenic: occurrence in groundwater." *Encyclopedia of environmental health* 2:1e17.

Chakraborti, Dipankar, Subhash C Mukherjee, Shyamapada Pati, Mrinal K Sengupta, Mohammad M Rahman, Uttam K Chowdhury, Dilip Lodh, Chitta R Chanda, Anil K Chakraborti, and Gautam K Basu. 2003. "Arsenic groundwater contamination in Middle Ganga Plain, Bihar, India: a future danger?" *Environmental Health Perspectives* 111 (9):1194-1198.

Chakraborti, Dipankar, Sushant K Singh, Mohammad Mahmudur Rahman, Rathindra Nath Dutta, Subhas Chandra Mukherjee, Shyamapada Pati, and Probir Bijoy Kar. 2018. "Groundwater arsenic contamination in the Ganga River Basin: a future health danger." *International Journal of Environmental Research and Public Health* 15 (2):180.

Fares, Ali, and Sushant K Singh. 2020. *Arsenic Water Resources Contamination*: Springer.

Ghasemian, Bahareh, Himan Shahabi, Ataollah Shirzadi, Nadhir Al-Ansari, Abolfazl Jaafari, Marten Geertsema, Assefa M Melesse, Sushant K Singh, and Anuar Ahmad. 2022. "Application of a Novel Hybrid Machine Learning Algorithm in Shallow Landslide Susceptibility Mapping in a Mountainous Area." *Frontiers in Environmental Science*:657.

Nhu, Viet-Ha, Ataollah Shirzadi, Himan Shahabi, Sushant K Singh, Nadhir Al-Ansari, John J Clague, Abolfazl Jaafari, Wei Chen, Shaghayegh Miraki, and Jie Dou. 2020. "Shallow landslide susceptibility mapping: A comparison between logistic model tree, logistic regression, naïve bayes tree, artificial neural network, and support vector machine algorithms." *International Journal of Environmental Research and Public Health* 17 (8):2749.

Nhu, Viet-Ha, Danesh Zandi, Himan Shahabi, Kamran Chapi, Ataollah Shirzadi, Nadhir Al-Ansari, Sushant K Singh, Jie Dou, and Hoang Nguyen. 2020. "Comparison of support vector machine, Bayesian logistic regression, and alternating decision tree algorithms for shallow landslide susceptibility mapping along a mountainous road in the west of Iran." *Applied Sciences* 10 (15):5047.

Pham, Binh Thai, Abolfazl Jaafari, Indra Prakash, Sushant K Singh, Nguyen Kim Quoc, and Dieu Tien Bui. 2019. "Hybrid computational intelligence models for groundwater potential mapping." *Catena* 182:104101.

Pham, Binh Thai, Tran Van Phong, Mohammadtaghi Avand, Nadhir Al-Ansari, Sushant K Singh, Hiep Van Le, and Indra Prakash. 2020. "Improving voting feature intervals for spatial prediction of landslides." *Mathematical Problems in Engineering* 2020.

Pham, Binh Thai, Tran Van Phong, Trung Nguyen-Thoi, Kajori Parial, Sushant K. Singh, Hai-Bang Ly, Kien Trung Nguyen, Lanh Si Ho, Hiep Van Le, and Indra Prakash. 2022. "Ensemble modeling of landslide susceptibility using random subspace learner and different decision tree classifiers." *Geocarto International* 37 (3):735-757.

Pham, Binh Thai, Indra Prakash, Jie Dou, Sushant K Singh, Phan Trong Trinh, Hieu Trung Tran, Tu Minh Le, Tran Van Phong, Dang Kim Khoi, and Ataollah Shirzadi. 2020. "A novel hybrid approach of landslide susceptibility modelling using rotation forest ensemble and different base classifiers." *Geocarto International* 35 (12):1267-1292.

Pham, Binh Thai, Indra Prakash, Sushant K Singh, Ataollah Shirzadi, Himan Shahabi, and Dieu Tien Bui. 2019. "Landslide susceptibility modeling using Reduced Error Pruning Trees and different ensemble techniques: Hybrid machine learning approaches." *Catena* 175:203-218.

Pham, Binh Thai, Sushant K Singh, and Hai-Bang Ly. 2020. "Using Artificial Neural Network (ANN) for prediction of soil." *Vietnam Journal of Earth Sciences* 42 (4):311-319.

Pham, Binh Thai, Tran Van Phong, Trung Nguyen-Thoi, Phan Trong Trinh, Quoc Cuong Tran, Lanh Si Ho, Sushant K Singh, Tran Thi Thanh Duyen, Loan Thi Nguyen, and Huy Quang Le. 2020. "GIS-based ensemble soft computing models for landslide susceptibility mapping." *Advances in Space Research* 66 (6):1303-1320.

Phong, Tran Van, Trong Trinh Phan, Indra Prakash, Sushant K Singh, Ataolla Shirzadi, Kamran Chapi, Hai-Bang Ly, Lanh Si Ho, Nguyen Kim Quoc, and Binh Thai Pham. 2021. "Landslide susceptibility modeling using different artificial intelligence methods: A case study at Muong Lay district, Vietnam." *Geocarto International* 36 (15):1685-1708.

Prasad, Priyanka, Sushant Kumar Singh, Sukanya Ghosh, Suchisnigdha Dutta, and Dona Sinha. 2022. "Influence of differential arsenic exposure on cellular redox homeostasis of exposed rural women of West Bengal." *Environmental Science and Pollution Research*:1-15.

Priyadarshini, Subhra. 2014. How the arsenic-affected perceive risk.

Shirzadi, Ataollah, Himan Shahabi, Kamal Nabiollahi, Ruhollah Taghizadeh-Mehrjardi, Ivan Lizaga, John J Clague, Sushant K Singh, Fariba Golmohamadi, and Anuar Ahmad. 2022. "Towards Robust Smart Data-Driven Soil Erodibility Index Prediction under Different Scenarios." *Geocarto International* (just-accepted):1-29.

Siegel, Peter E, John G Jones, Deborah M Pearsall, Nicholas P Dunning, Pat Farrell, Neil A Duncan, Jason H Curtis, and Sushant K Singh. 2015. "Paleoenvironmental evidence for first human colonization of the eastern Caribbean." *Quaternary Science Reviews* 129:275-295.

Siegel, Peter E, John G Jones, Deborah M Pearsall, Nicholas P Dunning, Pat Farrell, Neil A Duncan, Jason H Curtis, and Sushant K Singh. 2018. "Humanizing the landscapes of the Lesser Antilles during the Archaic Age." In *The Archaeology of Caribbean and Circum-Caribbean Farmers (6000 bc–ad 1500)*, 55-70. Routledge.

Singh, SK. 2011. "Arsenic contamination in water, soil, and food materials in Bihar." *LAP LAMBERT Academic Publishing, Germany*.

Singh, S.K., 2019. A career in environmental informatics and environmental data science. Frontiers in Ecology and the Environment, 17(4), pp.240-241.

Singh, SK, AK Ghosh, A Kumar, K Kislay, C Kumar, RR Tiwari, R Parwez, N Kumar, and MD Imam. 2014. "Groundwater arsenic contamination and associated health risks in Bihar, India." *International Journal of Environmental Research* 8 (1):49-60.

Singh, SK, GD Sanchez, and SK Panigrahi. 2014. "Multiple groundwater contamination in the Mid-Gangetic Plain, Bihar (India): a potential threat." *Int J Adv Res Sci Tech* 3 (3):175-179.

Singh, Sushant, Charles Feldman, and Shahla Wunderlich. 2014a. "Disaster issues and management in farm and urban crop production." *Perspectives in Public Health* 134 (3):127.

Singh, Sushant, Charles Feldman, and Shahla Wunderlich. 2014b. "Food Studies."

Singh, Sushant K. 2015a. "Groundwater arsenic contamination in the Middle-Gangetic Plain, Bihar (India): the danger arrived." *Int Res J Environ Sci* 4 (2):70-76.

Singh, Sushant K. 2016. "Geospatial analysis of census data for targeting new businesses using geoeconomics." *Journal of Intelligence Studies in Business* 6 (12):5-12.

Singh, Sushant K. 2017a. "An analysis of the cost-effectiveness of arsenic mitigation technologies: Implications for public policy." *International Journal of Sustainable Built Environment* 6 (2):522-535.

Singh, Sushant K. 2017b. "Conceptual framework of a cloud-based decision support system for arsenic health risk assessment." *Environment Systems and Decisions* 37 (4):435-450.

Singh, Sushant K. 2017c. "Evaluating two freely available geocoding tools for geographical inconsistencies and geocoding errors." *Open Geospatial Data, Software and Standards* 2 (1):1-8.

Singh, Sushant K. 2019. "A career in environmental informatics and environmental data science." *Frontiers in Ecology and the Environment* 17 (4):240-241.

Singh, Sushant K. 2020. "COVID-19: A master stroke of Nature." *AIMS Public Health* 7 (2):393.

Singh, Sushant, K , and AK Ghosh. 2010. "Effect of Arsenic on Photosynthesis, Growth and its Accumulation in the Tissues of Allium cepa (Onion)." *International Journal of Environmental Engineering and Management* 1 (1):39-50.

Singh, Sushant K, Stefanie A Brachfeld, and Robert W Taylor. 2016. "Evaluating hydrogeological and topographic controls on groundwater arsenic contamination in the Middle-Ganga plain in India: towards developing sustainable arsenic mitigation models." In *Emerging Issues in Groundwater Resources*, 263-287. Springer.

Singh, Sushant K, Ataollah Shirzadi, and Binh Thai Pham. 2021. "Application of artificial intelligence in predicting groundwater contaminants." *Water Pollution and Management Practices*:71-105.

Singh, Sushant K, and Eric A Stern. 2017. "Global arsenic contamination: living with the poison nectar." *Environment: Science and Policy for Sustainable Development* 59 (2):24-28.

Singh, Sushant K, and Robert W Taylor. 2019. "Assessing the role of risk perception in ensuring sustainable arsenic mitigation." *Groundwater for Sustainable Development* 9:100241.

Singh, Sushant K, and Robert W Taylor. 2020. "Assessing and Mapping Human Health Risks Due to Arsenic and Socioeconomic Correlates for Proactive Arsenic Mitigation." In *Arsenic Water Resources Contamination*, 231-256. Springer.

Singh, Sushant K, Robert W Taylor, Biswajeet Pradhan, Ataollah Shirzadi, and Binh Thai Pham. 2022. "Predicting sustainable arsenic mitigation using machine learning techniques." *Ecotoxicology and Environmental Safety* 232:113271.

Singh, Sushant K, Robert W Taylor, Mohammad Mahmudur Rahman, and Biswajeet Pradhan. 2018. "Developing robust arsenic awareness prediction models using machine learning algorithms." *Journal of Environmental Management* 211:125-137.

Singh, Sushant K, Robert W Taylor, and Haiyan Su. 2017. "Developing sustainable models of arsenic-mitigation technologies in the Middle-Ganga Plain in India." *Current Science*:80-93.

Singh, Sushant K, Robert W Taylor, and Venkatamallu Thadaboina. 2022. "Evaluating and predicting social behavior of arsenic affected communities: Towards developing arsenic resilient society." *Emerging Contaminants* 8:1-8.

Singh, Sushant K, and Neeraj Vedwan. 2015. "Mapping composite vulnerability to groundwater arsenic contamination: an analytical framework and a case study in India." *Natural Hazards* 75 (2):1883-1908.

Singh, Sushant Kumar. 2015b. *Assessing and mapping vulnerability and risk perceptions to groundwater arsenic contamination: Towards developing sustainable arsenic mitigation models*: Montclair State University.

Singh, Sushant Kumar, and Ashok Kumar Ghosh. 2011. "Entry of arsenic into food material—a case study." *World Appl Sci J* 13 (2):385-390.

Singh, Sushant Kumar, and Ashok Kumar Ghosh. 2012. "Health risk assessment due to groundwater arsenic contamination: children are at high risk." *Human and ecological risk assessment: An International Journal* 18 (4):751-766.

Thai Pham, B, I Prakash, J Dou, SK Singh, PT Trinh, H Trung Tran, T Minh Le, VP Tran, D Kim Khoi, and A Shirzadi. 2018.

"A novel hybrid approach of landslide susceptibility modeling using rotation forest ensemble and different base classifiers." *Geocarto Int* 14:1-38.

Tien Bui, Dieu, Ataollah Shirzadi, Ata Amini, Himan Shahabi, Nadhir Al-Ansari, Shahriar Hamidi, Sushant K Singh, Binh Thai Pham, Baharin Bin Ahmad, and Pezhman Taherei Ghazvinei. 2020. "A hybrid intelligence approach to enhance the prediction accuracy of local scour depth at complex bridge piers." *Sustainability* 12 (3):1063.

APPENDICES

Appendix-I: Research Profile

a) ORCID: https://orcid.org/0000-0001-6065-6050

b) ResearchGate: https://www.researchgate.net/profile/Sushant-Singh-10

c) Web of Science: https://www.webofscience.com/wos/author/record/G-5007-2015

d) Scopus: https://www.scopus.com/authid/detail.uri?authorId=56175892600

e) Vidwan: https://vidwan.inflibnet.ac.in/profile/132743

f) Loop: https://loop.frontiersin.org/people/893641/overview

g) Scihorizon: https://www.scihorizon.com/RID-20222862

h) AD Scientific Index: https://www.adscientificindex.com/scientist/sushant-k-singh/4345658

i) Selected Works: https://works.bepress.com/sushant-singh/

j) Amazon: https://www.amazon.com/author/sushantsingh

k) Personal website: https://sushantsingh.com/

Appendix-II Publications and Presentations

PUBLICATIONS

Edited Volumes

Sl. No.	Year	Publication
1	2020	Fares, A. and **Singh, S. K.** *Arsenic Water Resources Contamination - Challenges and Solutions.* Springer International Publishing, Springer Nature Switzerland AG. DOI: https://doi.org/10.1007/978-3-030-21258-2.

Books

Sl. No.	Year	Publication
1	2011	**Singh, S. K.** *Arsenic Contamination in Water, Soil, and Food Materials in Bihar.* Lambert Academic Publishing, Germany. ISBN 978-3-8443-2099-2.
2	2003	*Environment in Everyday Life.* Sustainable Development Forum, Institution of Engineers, India.

Refereed Journal Articles

Sl. No.	Year	Publication
1	2023	Prasad, P., **Singh, S.K.**, Ghosh, S., Dutta, S., Sinha, D. Influence of Differential Arsenic Exposure on Cellular Redox Homeostasis of Exposed Rural Women of West Bengal. *Environmental Science and Pollution Research, 30(3), 7836-7850*. DOI: https://doi.org/10.1007/s11356-022-22657-x. IF: 5.190.
2	2023	Singh, P., Sur, U., Rai, P. K., and Singh, S.K. Landslide susceptibility prediction using frequency ratio model: a case study of Uttarakhand, Himalaya (India). *Proceedings of the Indian National Science Academy.* DOI: https://doi.org/10.1007/s43538-023-00171-z.
3	2022	**Singh, S.K.** Genotoxic Effects of Arsenic in Food-Crops: A Need for Transgenerational Studies. *Journal of Clinical & Biomedical Research, 4(4), 1-5.* DOI: https://doi.org/10.47363/JCBR/2022(4)151.

4	2022	Ghasemian, B., Shahabi, H., Shirzadi, A., Al-Ansari, N., Jaafari, A., Geertsema, M., Melesse, A., **Singh, S.K.** and Ahmad, A., Application of Novel Hybrid Machine Learning Algorithm in Shallow Landslide Susceptibility Mapping in a Mountain Area. *Frontiers in Environmental Science, 10, 1-14*. DOI: https://doi.org/10.3389/fenvs.2022.897254. IF: 5.411.
5	2022	Shirzadi, A., Shahabi, H., Nabiollahi, K., Taghizadeh-Mehrjardi, R., Lizaga, I., Clague, J.J., **Singh, S.K.**, Golmohamadi, F. and Ahmad, A., 2022. Towards Robust Smart Data-Driven Soil Erodibility Index Prediction under Different Scenarios. *Geocarto International*, 1-34. DOI: https://doi.org/10.1080/10106049.2022.2076918. IF: 3.450.
6	2022	**Singh, S. K.,** Taylor, R. W., Pradhan, B., Shirzadi, A., and Pham, B.T. Predicting sustainable arsenic mitigation using machine learning techniques. *Ecotoxicology and Environmental Safety,* 232, 1-12. DOI: https://doi.org/10.1016/j.ecoenv.2022.113271. IF: 10.1.

7	2022	**Singh, S. K.,** Taylor, R. W., & Thadaboina, V. Evaluating and predicting social behavior of arsenic affected communities: Towards developing arsenic resilient society. *Emerging Contaminants*, 8, 1-8. DOI: https://doi.org/10.1016/j.emcon.2021.12.001. IF: 6.5.
8	2020	Pham, B.T., Phong, T.V., Avand, M.D., Al-Ansari, N. Singh, S.K., Le, H.V., and Prakash, I. Improving Voting Feature Intervals for Spatial Prediction of Landslides. *Mathematical Problems in Engineering,* 2020, 1-15. DOI: https://doi.org/10.1155/2020/4310791. IF: 1.430.
9	2020	Nhu, V.H., Zandi, D., Shahabi, H., Chapi, K., Shirzadi, A., Al-Ansari, N., **Singh, S.K.,** Dou, J., Nguyen, H. Comparison of Support Vector Machine, Bayesian Logistic Regression, and Alternating Decision Tree Algorithms for Shallow Landslide Susceptibility Mapping along a Mountainous Road in the West of Iran. *Applied Sciences,* 10(15), 5047. DOI: https://doi.org/10.3390/app10155047. IF: 2.838

10	2020	Pham, B.T., Phong, T.V., Thoia, T.N., Trinh, P.T., Tran, T.C., Ho, L.S., **Singh, S.K.**, Duyen, T.T.H., Nguyen, L.T., Le, H.Q., Le, H.P., Han, N.T.B., Quoc, N.K., Prakash, I. GIS-Based Ensemble Soft Computing Models for Landslide Susceptibility Mapping. *Advances in Space Research*, 66(6), 1303-1320. DOI: https://doi.org/10.1016/j.asr.2020.05.016. IF: 2.611.
11	2020	**Singh, S.K.** COVID-19: A Masterstroke of Nature. *AIMS Public Health, 2020, 7(2): 393-402.* DOI: https://doi.org/10.3934/publichealth.2020033.
12	2020	**Singh, S.K.** Global decision support dashboard of COVID-19. *AIMS Medical Science*, 7(2): 40-42. DOI: https://doi.org/15625/0866-7187/0/0/15008.
13	2020	**Singh, S.K.** A commentary on the Application of Artificial Intelligence in the Insurance Industry. *Trends in Artificial Intelligence*, 4(1):75-79. DOI: https://doi.org/10.36959/643/305.
14	2020	Pham, B.T., **Singh, S.K.** and Ly, H.B. Using Artificial Neural Network (ANN) for prediction of soil coefficient of consolidation. *Vietnam Journal of Earth Sciences*, 42(4), 311-319. DOI: https://doi.org/10.15625/0866-7187/0/0/15008. IF: 1.87.

15	2020	Pham, B.T., Phong, T.V., Nguyen-Thoi, T., Parial, K., **Singh, S.K.**, Ly, H.B., Nguyen, K.T., Ho, L.S., Le, H.V. and Prakash, I. Ensemble modeling of landslide susceptibility using random subspace learner and different decision tree classifiers. *Geocarto International*, 37(3), 735-757. DOI: https://doi.org/10.1080/10106049.2020.1737972. IF: 3.450.
16	2020	Nhu, V.H., Shirzadi, A., Shahabi, H., **Singh, S.K.**, Al-Ansari, N., Clague, J.J., Jaafari, A., Chen, W., Miraki, S., Dou, J. and Luu, C., 2020. Shallow Landslide Susceptibility Mapping: A Comparison between Logistic Model Tree, Logistic Regression, Naïve Bayes Tree, Artificial Neural Network, and Support Vector Machine Algorithms. *International Journal of Environmental Research and Public Health*, 17(8), p.2749. DOI: https://doi.org/10.3390/ijerph17082749. IF: 4.614.
17	2020	Bui, D.T., Shirzadi, A., Amini, A., Shahabi, H., Al-Ansari, N., Hamidi, S., **Singh, S.K.**, Thai Pham, B., Ahmad, B.B. and Ghazvinei, P.T., 2020. A Hybrid Intelligence Approach to Enhance the Prediction Accuracy of Local Scour Depth at Complex Bridge Piers. *Sustainability*, 12(3), p.1063. DOI: https://doi.org/10.3390/su12031063. IF: 3.889.

18	2019	Pham, B.T.; Shirzadi, A.; Shahabi, H.; Omidvar, E.; **Singh, S.K.**; Sahana, M.; Asl, D.T.; Ahmad, B.B.; Quoc, N.K.; Lee, S. Landslide Susceptibility Assessment by Novel Hybrid Machine Learning Algorithms. *Sustainability, 11(16), 4386.* DOI: https://doi.org/10.3390/su11164386. IF: 3.889.
19	2019	Phong, T.V., Phan, T.T., Prakash, I., **Singh, S.K.**, Shirzadi, A., Chapi, K., Ly, H.B., Ho, L.S., Quoc, N.K. and Pham, B.T. Landslide susceptibility modeling using different artificial intelligence methods: a case study at Muong Lay district, Vietnam. *Geocarto International, 36(15), 1685-1708.* DOI: https://doi.org/10.1080/10106049.2019.1665715. IF: 3.450.
20	2019	**Singh, S.K.** and Taylor, W. Assessing the role of risk perception in ensuring sustainable arsenic Mitigation. *Groundwater for Sustainable Development, 9, 1-14.* DOI: https://doi.org/10.1016/j.gsd.2019.100241. IF: 7.9.
21	2019	Jaafari, A., Pham, B.T., Prakash, I., **Singh, S.K.**, Bui, D.T. Hybrid computational intelligence models for groundwater potential mapping. *Catena, 182,1-13.* DOI: https://doi.org/10.1016/j.catena.2019.104101. IF: 6.367.

22	2019	**Singh, S. K.** A career in environmental informatics and environmental data science. *Frontiers in Ecology and the Environment.* 17 (4): 240-241. DOI: https://doi.org/10.1002/fee.2038. IF: 13.78.
23	2019	Pham B.T., Prakash I., **Singh S.K.,** Shirzadi A., Shahabi H., Bui D.T. Landslide susceptibility modeling using Reduced Error Pruning Trees and different ensemble techniques: Hybrid machine learning approaches. *Catena*, 175, 203-18. DOI: https://doi.org/10.1016/j.catena.2018.12.018. IF: 6.367.
24	2019	Pham B.T., Prakash I., Dou J, **Singh S.K.,** Trinh P.T., Trung T.H., Minh L.T., Tran V.P., Kim K. D., Shirzadi A., Tien B.D. A novel hybrid approach of landslide susceptibility modeling using rotation forest ensemble and different base classifiers. *Geocarto International*, 35(12), 1267-1292. DOI: https://doi.org/10.1080/10106049.2018.1559885. IF: 3.450.
25	2018	**Singh, S.K.,** Taylor, R.W., Rahman, M.M. and Pradhan, B. Developing robust arsenic awareness prediction models using machine learning algorithms. *Journal of Environmental Management. 211C: 125-137.* DOI: https://doi.org/10.1016/j.jenvman.2018.01.044. IF: 8.91.

26	2018	Chakraborti, D., **Singh, S.K.**, Rahman, M.M., Dutta, R.N., Mukherjee, S.C., Pati, S.K, and Probir, B. Groundwater Arsenic Contamination in the Ganga River Basin: A Future Health Danger. *International Journal of Environmental Research and Public Health*, 15(2): 180. DOI: https://doi.org/10.3390/ijerph15020180. IF: 4.614.
27	2017	**Singh, S. K.** An Analysis of the Cost-Effectiveness of Arsenic Mitigation Technologies: Implications for Public Policy. *International Journal of Sustainable Built Environment*, 6(2): 522-535. DOI: https://doi.org/10.1016/j.ijsbe.2017.10.004.
28	2017	**Singh, S.K.,** Taylor, R.W., and Su, H. Developing Sustainable Models of Arsenic-Mitigation Technologies in the Middle-Ganga Plain in India. *Current Science. 113(1): 80-93.* DOI: https://doi.org/10.18520/cs/v113/i01/80-93. IF: 1.102.
29	2017	**Singh, S. K.** Conceptual Framework of a Cloud-based Decision Support System for Arsenic Health Risk Assessment. *Environment Systems and Decisions.* 37(4): 435-450. DOI: https://doi.org/10.1007/s10669-017-9641-x.

30	2017	**Singh, S. K.** Evaluating Two Open Source Geocoding Tools for Geographical Inconsistencies of Geocoding Errors. *Open Geospatial Data, Software and Standards*, 2(1), 1-8. DOI: https://doi.org/10.1186/s40965-017-0026-3.
31	2017	**Singh, S.K.** and Stern, E.A. Global Arsenic Contamination: Living with the Poison Nectar. *Environment: Science and Policy for Sustainable Development,* 59(2): 24-28. DOI: https://doi.org/10.1080/00139157.2017.1274583. IF: 4.108.
32	2016	**Singh, S. K.** Geospatial analysis of census data for targeting new businesses using Geoeconomics. *Journal of Intelligence Studies in Business.* 6(3): 5-12. IF: 0.29.
33	2015	Siegel, Peter E., John G. Jones, Deborah M. Pearsall, Nicholas P. Dunning, Pat Farrell, Neil A. Duncan, Jason H. Curtis, and **Singh, S.K.** Paleoenvironmental Evidence for First Human Colonization of the Eastern Caribbean. *Quaternary Science Reviews,* 129(December 1):275-295. DOI: https://doi.org/10.1016/j.quascirev.2015.10.014. IF: 4.456.

34	2015	**Singh, S.K.** and Vedwan, N. Mapping Composite Vulnerability to Groundwater Arsenic Contamination: An Analytical Framework and a Case Study in India. *Natural Hazards*, 75(2): 1883-1908. DOI: https://doi.org/10.1007/s11069-014-1402-2. IF: 3.158.
35	2014	**Singh, S. K.** Groundwater Arsenic Contamination in the Middle-Gangetic Plain, Bihar (India): The Danger Arrived. *International Research Journal of Environmental Sciences,* 4(2): 70-76.
36	2014	**Singh, S.K.,** Gin D. Sanchez, and Panigrahi, S.K. Multiple Groundwater Contamination in the Mid-Gangetic Plain, Bihar (India): A Potential Threat. *International Journal of Advanced Research in Science and Technology,* 3(3): 175-179.
37	2014	**Singh, S.K.,** Feldman, C., & Wunderlich, S. Heavy Metal Contamination in Vegetables Grown in an Urban Community Garden in the Northeast USA: A Preliminary Study. *Food Studies: An Interdisciplinary Journal,* 3(3): 77-87. DOI: https://doi.org/10.18848/2160-1933/CGP/v03i03/40582.

38	2014	**Singh, S.K,** Feldman, C., & Wunderlich, S. Disaster Issues and Management in Farm and Urban Crop Production. *Perspectives in Public Health*, 134(3): 127-128. DOI: https://doi.org/10.1177/1757913914530844. IF: 3.627.
39	2014	**Singh, S.K.,** Ghosh, A.K., Kumar, A., Kislay, A., Kumar, C., Tiwari, R.R., Parwez, R., Kumar, N., Imam, M.D. Groundwater Arsenic Contamination and Associated Health Risks in Bihar, India. *International Journal of Environmental Research*, 8(1): 49-60. https://doi.org/10.22059/IJER.2014.693. IF: 3.229.
40	2012	**Singh, S.K.** and Ghosh, A.K. Health Risk Assessment due to Ground Water Arsenic Contamination-Children are at High Risk. *Human and Ecological Risk Assessment: An International Journal,* 18(4): 751-766. DOI: https://doi.org/10.1080/10807039.2012.688700. IF: 4.997.
41	2011	**Singh, S.K.** and Ghosh, A.K. Entry of Arsenic into Food Material - A Case Study. *World Applied Science Journal,* 13(2): 385-390. IF: 0.6.

| 42 | 2010 | **Singh, S.K.** and Ghosh, A.K. Effect of Arsenic on Photosynthesis, Growth, and its Accumulation in the Tissues of *Allium cepa* (Onion). *International Journal of Environmental Engineering and Management*, 1(1): 39-50. |

Book Chapters

Sl. No.	Year	Publication
1	2021	**Singh, S.K.**, Shirzadi, A., and Pham, B.T. Application of Artificial Intelligence in Predicting Groundwater Contaminants. In Singh, A., Agrawal, M., and Agrawal, S.B. *Water Pollution and Management Practices.* Springer International Publishing, Springer Nature Switzerland AG. DOI: https://doi.org/10.1007/978-981-15-8358-2_4.
2	2019	**Singh, S.K.** and Taylor, R.W. Assessing and mapping human health risks due to arsenic and socioeconomic correlates for proactive arsenic Mitigation. In A. Fares and Singh, S.K. (eds.), *Advances in Water Security: Arsenic Water Resources Contamination - Challenges and Solutions.* Springer International Publishing, Springer Nature Switzerland AG. DOI: https://doi.org/10.1007/978-3-030-21258-2_10.

3	2016	**Singh, S.K.**, Brachfeld, S.A., and Taylor, R.W. Evaluating hydrogeological and topographic controls on groundwater arsenic contamination in the mid-Gangetic Plain in India: Towards Developing Sustainable Arsenic Mitigation Models. In A. Fares (ed.), *Advances in Water Security: Emerging Sensing Issues for Coastal Groundwater Quality and Quantity*. Springer International Publishing, New York, USA. DOI: https://doi.org/10.1007/978-3-319-32008-3, 263-287.
4	2011	**Singh, S.K.** Are Western Values, Ethics, and Dominant Paradigms Compatible with Sustainability? - Issue-3. In *Taking Sides: Clashing Views on Sustainability*. Robert W. Taylor. McGraw-Hill (ed.), ISBN: 0073514500 / 9780073514505.
5	2009	Ghosh, A.K., Singh, S.K., Bose, N., **Singh, S.K.**, Roy, N.P., Upadhyaya, A. Arsenic Hotspots detected in the state of Bihar (India) a serious health hazards for estimated human population of 5.5 Lakh. In *Assessment of Ground Water Resources and Management*, Ramanathan, A.L., Bhattacharya, P., Keshari, P.K., Bundschuh, J., Chandrashekharam, D., and Singh, S.K. (Eds.) I. K. International Publishing House Pvt. Ltd., New Delhi, ISBN: 978-81-906757-2-7, 62-70.

Encyclopedia Entries

Sl. No.	Year	Publication
1	2017	Chakraborti, D. **Singh, S.K.**, Rashid, H.M. and Rahman, M.M. Arsenic: occurrence in groundwater. *Encyclopedia of Environmental Health. Burlington: Elsevier,* *2: 1-17.* DOI: https://doi.org/10.1016/ B978-0-12-409548-9.10634-7.

Conference Proceedings

Sl. No.	Year	Publication
1	2019	**Singh, S.K.** and Taylor, W. Likelihood of adoption of arsenic-mitigation technologies under perceived risks to health, income, and social discrimination to arsenic contamination. Zhu Y, Guo H, Bhattacharya P, Ahmad A, Bundschuh J, Naidu R. *Environmental Arsenic in a Changing World: Proceedings of the 7th International Congress and Exhibition on Arsenic in the Environment (AS 2018)*, July 1-6, 2018, Beijing, PR China. CRC Press; 2019 Apr 15.

| 2 | 2007 | Bose, N., Ghosh, A.K., Roy, N.P., Upadhyay, A., Singh, A., **Singh, S.K.** Vulnerability of Population Exposed to Arsenic Contamination in the Mid-Ganga Plain of Bihar (India). *Annual Conference of Royal Geographical Society (RGS-IBG – AC-07)*, London, U.K, August 28-31. |
| 3 | 2007 | Ghosh, A. K., S. K. Singh, N. Bose, **Singh, S.K.**, A. Singh, S. Chaudhary, R. Mishra, N. P. Roy, and A. Upadhyay. Study of Arsenic Contamination in Ground Water of Bihar (India) Along the River Ganges. *International Workshop on Arsenic Sourcing and Mobilisation in Holocene Deltas*. K.P. Basu Memorial Hall at Jadavpur University, Kolkata, India, School of Fundamental Research, Kolkata, India. December 12-13. |

INVITED TALKS

Sl. No.	Year	Talk
1	2022	Application of Artificial Intelligence in Environmental Management and Sustainability. Annual Tech Fest " PANTHEON": "Technological Advancement in Environmental Mitigation," organized by Birla Institute of Technology, Mesra, Ranchi-835215, Jharkhand, India.

2	2021	Artificial Intelligence and its Application in Various Domains. GURU DAKSHTA 7th Faculty Induction Programme Organized by office of the Director UGC- Human Resource Development Centre Morabadi Campus, Ranchi University, Ranchi – 834008 (Jharkhand). December 22, 2021.
3	2021	Achieving the Sustainable Development Goals using Artificial Intelligence as a Keynote speaker in One Day International Webinar on "Growing Impact of Ethical and Trusted Artificial Intelligence/ML in Public Health Care Systems" organized by Anugrah Memorial College, Gaya, Magadh University, Bihar, India. September 29, 2021.
4	2021	Application of artificial intelligence in environmental sustainability, Analytics Conference: Exploring Career in Data Analytics, Moore Statistics Consulting LLC, USA. March 16-18, 2021.
5	2020	A Machine Learning Approach to Solve Groundwater Arsenic Contamination Challenges. Shyama Prasad Mukherjee University, Ranchi, Jharkhand, India. September 9, 2020.

6	2020	Application of Machine Learning in Environmental Management. A. N. College, Patna, Patliputra University, Bihar, India. June 27, 2020.
7	2019	Application of Artificial Intelligence in Sustainable Arsenic Mitigation. Flame University, Department of Economics. November 7, 2019.
8	2013	Arsenic in the Food chain and Social Vulnerability in the Eastern State of India. Arsenic Mitigation in Ganges-Brahmaputra Delta. NWO WOTRO Urbanizing Deltas of the World. Patna, India, August 17-18.
9	2009	Impact of Climate Change and role of Community in its Mitigation. 'Creating a Healthy Society with a focus on Climate Change, Health and Environment,' UNESCO and WHO, Patna, India, November 16-18.
10	2009	Dying Ganga-Human Beings are the Killers. 'Water Conservation Day' organized by Yuvsatta (NGO), Ministry of Water Resources, Government of India, Chandigarh, India, September 27-October 1.

| 11 | 2008 | Climatic Change Mitigation and Sustainable Development. Indian Youth Summit on Climate Change- Intergenerational Partnerships for Climate Change Mitigation and Adaptation. Visthar, Bangalore, India, April 22-25. |

POLICY INPUTS

Sl. No.	Year	Contribution
1	2009	Core team member: Mid-Day-Meal Plan, Government of Bihar, India.
2	2006	Primary author: Status of Primary Education in Patna Urban-6, Ministry of Human Resource Development, Government of Bihar, India.
3	2004	Core team member: National Biodiversity Strategy and Action Plan for Bihar, India.
4	2003	Core team member: State of Environment Report, Bihar, India.

CONFERENCE ACTIVITY

Seminars/Workshops/Symposia Organized

Sl. No.	Year	Topic
1	2014	Geogenic Arsenic in The Soils and Aquifers: Causes and Environmental Impacts in the EGU-SSS conference on "The Earth Living Skin: Soil, Life, and Climate Changes." Bari, Italy, September 22–25.

2	2009	International Seminar on 'Environmental Degradation and Remediation,' Department of Environment and Water Management, Anugrah Narayan College, Patna and Scientific Foresight at Patna, India, February 20.
3	2008	International Conference' Scientific foresight,' Sri Krishna Memorial Hall, Patna, India, December 22-24.
4	2007	International conference 'Scientific Foresight,' Department of Science and Technology, Government of Patna, India, December 22-24.
5	2006	Workshop on 'Bihar Vision-2015 for Socioeconomic development and Productivity Enhancement,' Bihar State Productivity Council and Indian National Trade Union Congress, Patna, India, October 22.
6	2006	Workshop on 'Investing in Agriculture for Food Security,' Bihar State Productivity Council, Patna, India, October 16.
7	2005	International seminar on 'Cleaner Production Technology (C.P.),' Anugrah Narayan College, Magadh University, Patna, India, November 29.

8	2003	International Conference on 'Urban Waste Management-Present and Future,' Department of Environment and Water Management, Anugrah Narayan College, Magadh University, Patna, India, December 15.

Paper Presentation

Sl. No.	Year	Topic
1	2018	Application of Artificial Intelligence in Environmental Modelling and Sustainability. European Congress on Applied Science and Innovative Engineering. Athens, Greece, 12-13 November. DOI: 10.21767/2394-9988-C1-002.
2	2018	Likelihood of adoption of arsenic-mitigation technologies under perceived risks to health, income, and social discrimination to arsenic contamination, w/ Taylor, R.W. 7th International Congress & Exhibition on Arsenic in the Environment, Environmental Arsenic in a Changing World. Beijing, P. R. China 1-6 July.
3	2018	Predicting the Most Preferred Sustainable Arsenic Mitigation Technology using Machine Learning Algorithms, w/ Taylor, R.W., and Binh Thai Pham. RGS-IBG Annual International Conference, Cardiff University, U.K., August 28-31.

4	2015	Sustainable Arsenic Mitigation Framework: A Methodological Approach Towards an Arsenic Resilient Society. "Arsenic Contamination of Groundwater in Middle Ganga Plain of Bihar: Issues, Concerns, and Remedial Measures." Central Ground Water Authority & Central Ground Water Board Mid- Eastern Region, Ministry of Water Resources, R.D. & G.R. Government of India, Patna, March 25.
5	2015	Assessing and Mapping Groundwater Contamination for Creating and Prioritizing Mitigation Policies, w/ Gin D. Sanchez, and Panigrahi, S.K. Association of American Geographers Annual Meeting, Chicago, IL, April 21-25.
6	2015	Application of Remote Sensing and GIS in Water Resources Management: A Case Study in the Mid-Gangetic Plain in India, w/Ahmad, M.Y. Association of American Geographers Annual Meeting, Chicago, IL, April 21-25.
7	2014	Application of Risk Perception in Decision-making for Sustainable Arsenic Mitigation. University Student Research Symposium, Montclair State University, NJ, April 12.

8	2014	Role of Risk Perception in Decision Making for Arsenic Mitigation, w/ Vedwan, N. Society for Applied Anthropology Annual Meeting, Albuquerque, NM, March 18-22.
9	2013	Developing a Socioeconomic Model of Sustainable Arsenic Mitigation: A Case Study of Bihar, India. Sustainability Seminar Series, Department of Earth and Environmental Studies. Montclair State University, NJ, April 16.
10	2013	Groundwater Arsenic Contamination in Eastern India: A Composite Vulnerability Approach to Assessing Risk and Adaptation, w/ Vedwan, N. Society for Applied Anthropology: Natural Resource Distribution and Development in the 21st Century. Denver, CO, March 19-23.
11	2009	Arsenic in Food Chain-A New threat to inhabitants of Bihar, w/ Ghosh, A.K.' Geogenic Contamination of Ground Water, Government of India, Ministry of Water Resources, Central Ground Water Board, Mid-Eastern Region, Patna, India., March 21-22.

12	2008	Water and Sanitation-Constraints and Solution. Seminar on 'Citizen's Report on Domestic Water and Sanitation-Consultation Meeting,' Water Aid India and Department of Environment and Water Management, Anugrah Narayan College, Magadh University, Patna, India, August 6.
13	2007	**Singh, S.K.**, Ghosh, A.K., Singh, S., Shankar, V. Arsenic Contamination in Ground Water with special reference to Bihar. National Seminar sponsored by the University Grants Commission, India, organized by L. P. Shahi College, Patna, Magadh University, India, July 14-15.
14	2007	Shankar, V., **Singh, S.K.**, Ghosh, A.K., Singh, S. Study on Physico-Chemical Characteristics of Flowing Water of Ganges River at Mokamah. University Grants Commission, India sponsored National Seminar organized by L. P. Shahi College, Patna, Magadh University, India, July 14-15.
15	2007	Bose, N., Ghosh, A.K., Roy, N.P., Upadhyay, A., Singh, A., and **Singh, S.K.** Vulnerability of Population Exposed to Arsenic Contamination in the Mid-Ganga Plain of Bihar (India). Annual Conference of Royal Geographical Society (RGS-IBG – AC-07), London, August 28-31.

| 16 | 2006 | Ghosh, A.K., Singh, S.K., Bose, N., Roy, N.P., **Singh, S.K.**, Singh, A., Upadhyay, A., and Kumar, Shailendra. Assessment of Arsenic Contamination in the Ground Water Sources of Ganga Floodplain of Bhojpur District, Bihar. International Conference- Groundwater for Sustainable Development Problems, Perspectives, and Challenges, Jawaharlal Nehru University New Delhi, India, February 1-4. |

Abstracts

Sl. No.	Year	Topic
1	2014	**Singh, S.K.**, Vedwan, N., and Thampi, A.P. Decision Support System for Vulnerability Assessment in Arsenic Contaminated Areas. The Earth Living Skin: Soil, Life, and Climate Changes. EGU – SSS Conference, Bari, Italy, September 22–25.
2	2014	**Singh, S.K.** and Vedwan, N. Socioeconomic Model of Arsenic Mitigation: A Case Study in India. Goldschmidt Conference. Sacramento, CA, June 8-13.
3	2009	**Singh, S.K.** and Bozzolasco, A. Arsenic Problem in India: an Environmental Justice Perspective. 11th Global Conference: Environmental Justice and Global Citizenship, Oxford, U.K., July 3-5.

4	2009	Ghosh, A.K., Singh, Shatrunjay K., Bose, N., and **Singh, S.K.** Monitoring and Management of Arsenic and Fluoride Contamination in Ground Water of Bihar. 31st Annual Conference of Bangladesh Chemical Society, University of Dhaka, Dhaka, Bangladesh, January 30-February 2.
5	2008	Ghosh, A.K., Bose, N., **Singh, S.K.,** and Bhatt, A.G. A comprehensive model for arsenic Mitigation in rural areas of developing economies. 2nd PRAMA workshop on Risk Assessment. The University of Manchester, U.K., June 23-25.
6	2008	Ghosh, A.K., Bose, N., and **Singh, S.K.** Emerging constraint in the mitigation strategies adopted in the Arsenic affected area of Bihar plain. 2nd International Congress, Arsenic in the Environment: Arsenic from Nature to Human. Valencia, Spain, May 21-23.
7	2007	Ghosh, A.K., Bose, N., **Singh, S.K.,** and Bhatt, A.G. A comprehensive model for arsenic Mitigation in rural areas of developing economies. 2nd PRAMA workshop on Risk Assessment. The University of Manchester, U.K., June 23-25.

Poster Presentation

Sl. No.	Year	Topic
1	2018	Lesion Localization and Classification in Mammograms Using Advanced Deep Learning Based on Retinanet, w/ Sharihahmadian, E., Feng, J., Strait, C, Gomathy, K.P., and Swami, M. Big Data and Cancer Precision Medicine Conference, organized by Dana-Farber Cancer Institute, cBio Center at Dana-Farber, Nature, Nature Biotechnology and Nature Biomedical Engineering. Joseph B. Martin Conference Center, Boston, MA, USA October 1-2.
2	2013	**Singh, S.K.** and Ferdinand, A.V. Waterborne Diseases Prevention Priority Index (WDPPI): A Spatial Decision Support Tool. GIS for the United Nations and the International Community Conference (5219), New York, October 10-11.
3	2012	**Singh, S.K.** and Vedwan, N. Deriving a Social Vulnerability Scale for Arsenic Affected Areas in South Asia. Socio-Environmental Synthesis Education Workshop, National Socio-Environmental Synthesis Center (SESYNC), Annapolis, MD, June 4-5.

| 4 | 2011 | **Singh, S.K.** and Ghosh, A.K. Health Risk Assessment of Ground Water Arsenic Contamination in Bihar (India) and Related Socioeconomic Challenges. Students Research Symposium. Montclair State University, NJ, April 16. |
| 5 | 2010 | **Singh, S.K.** and Ghosh, A.K. Groundwater Arsenic Contamination in Maner (Patna) – Kids are at High Health Risk. The Unite For Sight Global Health and Innovation Conference.' Yale University, New Haven, CT, April 17-18. |

Appendix-III Reviewer and Editorial Experiences

Editorial Experience

Sl. No.	Journal
1	Associate Editor of Frontiers in Environmental Science: Big Data, AI, and the Environment
2	Associate Editor of Frontiers in Environmental Science: Toxicology, Pollution, and the Environment
3	Editor-in-Chief, Journal of Artificial Intelligence and Environmental Sustainability
4	Associate Editor, Food Studies: An Interdisciplinary Journal
5	Editorial Board Member, International Journal of Applied Environmental Sciences

6	Editorial Board Member, International Journal of Applied Engineering Research
7	Topic Editor: Electronics

Peer Reviewing Experience

Sl. No.	Journal	Impact Factor
1	Bulletin of the World Health Organization	9.408
2	Chemosphere	7.086
3	Economics & Human Biology	2.184
4	Environmental Science and Technology	11.357
5	Environmental Technology and Innovation	7.758
6	Environmental Science: Water Research & Technology	5.819
7	Human and Ecological Risk Assessment: An International Journal	5.2
8	International Journal of Environmental Science and Technology	2.860
9	International Journal of Environmental Research and Public Health	4.614
10	ISPRS international journal of geo-information	3.099
11	Journal of Cleaner Production	11.072

12	Journal of Trace Elements in Medicine and Biology	3.995
13	PLOS Computational Biology	4.779
14	Remote Sensing	5.349
15	Science of the Total Environment	10.754
16	Scientific Reports	4.996
17	Sustainability	3.889